By Contraries

AND OTHER POEMS

OTHER BOOKS BY MARK RUDMAN

Poetry

IN THE NEIGHBORING CELL   1982

Chapbooks:

THE RUIN REVIVED   1986

THE MYSTERY IN THE GARDEN   1985

Prose

ROBERT LOWELL: AN INTRODUCTION TO THE POETRY   1983

Translation

MY SISTER—LIFE and THE SUBLIME MALADY (Poems by Boris Pasternak with Bohdan Boychuk)   1982

SQUARE OF ANGELS: Selected Poems of Bohdan Antonych (with Bohdan Boychuk)   1977

Editor

SECRET DESTINATIONS: WRITERS ON TRAVEL   1985

MARK RUDMAN

By Contraries

AND OTHER POEMS

The National Poetry Foundation
University of Maine
Orono, Maine 04469

ACKNOWLEDGEMENTS

I want to thank the editors of the following journals where most of the poems in the book first appeared, often in earlier versions:

The American Poetry Review: "Address to the Analyst," *The Atlantic Monthly*: "Taken by Brown," "Family Romance," *Boulevard*: "Recovering from Michelangelo," "Maturity," *The California Quarterly*: "Scrapings" (1,2,9), *First Issue*: "The Dancing Party," *Harvard Magazine*: "The Blouse," "The Missing Delft," *Ironwood*: "By Contraries" (1-10), *The Kentucky Poetry Review*: "Waiting Out the End of Winter," *The Literary Review*: "Any One Bone You Want," *Modern Poetry Studies*: "Flying," *Origin*: "Enigma After The Dreadful Thunderclap," "Perspective," "The Pyre" (under the title "After A Death"), *The Paris Review*: "Abilene," "The Man in the Room," "Full Circle" (under the title "Solitaire"), "The Punch," *The Partisan Review*: "August Is Not A Month," "Cipher," *Pequod*: "A Reprieve," "At the Asian Star on the Eve of Another Departure," "Lines Written on the Via Veneto," "By Contraries" (19-23), *Ploughshares*: "Running Out," *Poetry East*: "Solstice," "Terrestrial Marks" (3, under the title "The Morning After"), "Orphanos," "Peripheral Vision," "Threshold," *The Southern Review*: "Scrapings" (4,5,6,11), *Telescope*: "Pictures at an Exhibition," *Tendril*: "The Gallery," *Trellis 2*: "In the Neighboring Cell," "Tomorrow They Will Mow the Cornfield," "Notes on 'In the Neighboring Cell'," *2Plus2*: "Milan," "Verticals," *The Virginia Quarterly*: "Signals," "The Black Dove"

Anthologies:

Academy of American Poets Anthology 1967-1972: "Scrapings" (8,9)
A Celebration for Stanley Kunitz, "The Mystery in the Garden"
The New Directions Annual 41: "Scrapings" (under the title "Salvagings"), "Homecoming," "Deer Isle and Voices"
The Random Review 1982: "Log (Journey to 'Four Corners')"
Secret Destinations: Writers on Travel: "Perspective," "Rome," "Recovering from Michelangelo," "First Glances," "Last Morning"

The sequence *The Ruin Revived* was published as a chapbook by Branden Press.

The Mystery in the Garden was published as a chapbook by Deborah Thomas (Spuyten Duyvil).

Thanks are also due to the Ingram-Merrill Foundation for a Fellowship, and to the Corporation of Yaddo where a number of these poems were written and revised.

Published by The National Poetry Foundation,
University of Maine, Orono, Maine 04469

Printed by The University of Maine Printing Office

Library of Congress Catalog Card Number: 86-64043
ISBN: 0-915032-92-9 cloth
ISBN: 0-915032-93-7 paper

Cover by Michael Flanagan

For Madelaine and Samuel

CONTENTS

3. POEMS 1981-1984

ONE

Now that you have broken through the wall with your head what will you do in the neighboring cell?

Stanislaw Jerzy Lec

THE FLOWERPOTS

I am watching the flowerpots
across the way. Only the resistance
of the air prevents them from toppling
onto some passing head. But in two years

none have fallen. I think of what it might
be like to sit there for years
without wavering from a fixed point.
And with something growing inside you!

THE DANCING PARTY

In the beginning nothing was out of place.

Then they let the children in.

The guests formed a ring
to enclose the children.

The ring would wriggle in and out.

When it wriggled in it was
to retrieve a child.

A blond   cherubic child
was the first chosen.

A man grabbed the child by the hips
and stuffed him into his mouth   slowly
savoring every inch of entry.

This was not my kind of party.

Beneath the music of digestion
my ears picked up the echo of footsteps.

Sounds drifted towards me.
I had not moved.

Sounds drew me through a waterfall of beads
into the neighboring room.

There was a party within a party
and all the attendants were women,
women of all ages,
women in white dancing costumes.

The women were dancing.
They danced to the beat of their footsteps.
At the end of a weaving line
one woman motioned me to join.

I'm a lousy dancer   I trip easily.
I did not want to dance.
I did not want to devour the children.

I joined the dance.

I fell   and fell again   and rose.

Bruises sprouted on my skin.

The step was too much to grasp   too soon.

I ceased to resist.
I let my feet go their own way.
My arms followed.

I was dancing,
feet and arms
faster than my feet,
left leg shot out
to the left,
right leg shot out
to the right,
left leg crossed over the right leg
crossed over the left,
the children dying,
the ring round as a ring around,
me dancing,
the women dancing,
the children dead,
the broken back of a kite in splinters,
confetti falling,
the men gulping everything,
refuse of children,
refuse of men,

erupting,
me turning,
mindless,
turning me　turning me
turning.

SCRAPINGS

1

Light from the hallway seeps under the door.
I wear the night over my eye like a patch.

I lock the doors. The walls close in.
The glaciers holler. I can't hear them.

What's conceived is barely spoken.
If it gets too dim, call it mist.

I pawned my brain in order to be reasonable.
The claim ticket's misplaced, not lost.

Inside the old house, thick with musk,
the walls of the matriarch are lined with mink.

2

I arrive at the station. The train is empty,
but cannot accommodate any more passengers.

Snow covers the tracks. A white animal pauses.
I touch my beard and my hand fills with snow.

The child hugs the doll, the doll hugs her back;
the child dies of shock and they bury the doll.

The matador pauses before the kill:
there is more to this flourish than show.

Choices bleed into acts: you sit at ringside,
but are no spectator, unless you can keep dry.

3

The perilous instant is blessed: witness the ant
scaling crevices on the butcher block counter.

Another seasonal shift: a pigeon's trapped
in the airshaft. Continual threat of avalanche.

I keep glancing at the calendar on my watch
wondering why it is so cold if it is nearly spring.

I hear the prisoners were asked to redesign the fortress
for the prevention of suicide in the death cell.

Clusters of galaxies in my coffee cup. One long sip and the rims
are smeared with the flotsam of exhausted stars.

4

No news to report, but yesterday a crack in the sky
became a scar on the cheek of heaven.

I do not believe in omens and yet my heart leapt at the sight
of an opossum in a death trance baring his pearly fangs at the
    moon.

The simple life eludes me: the autumn sky inside my head
is a sheet of lead, angelic and sinister.

Nightly I watch the same promiscuous commercial in muggy color.
My head throbs. One mistake and a life lost in the making.

To what can the spirit adhere? Old shoes with dirt sticking
to the soles: more simple things to blind us into saying yes.

5

On either side of the road there is danger: nameless beasts
that make strange moans and never show their faces.

I don't need you anymore to tell me which turn to take.
I can stomach pain; it is deceit that undoes me.

I know I have built my house with the bricks of anxiety
but to feel nothing hurts most in the long run.

The men that thought franchise was ownership left us hanging
upside down and went away singing the songs we taught them.

Five birds wing it out of one nest the size of a saucer.
And still they cart the night away in phosphorescent trucks.

6

I love this sodden landscape where tree, telephone pole
and plumbing combine to make a vast network of pulsations.

It begins on a map. You throw a dart.
It lands anywhere and blood comes out.

Fog: an unformed face, embryo of unknown
species that come and go with the weather.

The weather survives the weather: wingless, eye-
less, tongueless, it can't remember to forget.

The arena is empty: it is time for the spectators to die.
One instant of silence is louder than history's accumulated noise.

7

Only the solitaries are never alone,
their minds always filled with the image of another.

Between two distances I will have the nearest.
As long as I try to look at the wind I am deaf.

If only the hot plate had two burners
and didn't take an eternity to heat up.

Broadly speaking. Broadly? It's not what I meant.
All points are small enough to be missed.

The scent I lay down
does not lead me back to my tracks.

8

I survived the jump from the rooftop
but get mauled every time I play a guessing game.

You tear at me from the inside out,
a thick rope rubbing up and down my windpipe.

Waiting and waiting: a cloud of smoke in my lungs.
There is nothing between us but separation.

The walls of the prisons are coated with stamps.
I can no longer pretend that my bathtub is a lake.

I live under a leaking roof, and when it rains
I am forced to sleep with a bucket over my head.

9

My name was stuck onto me like masking tape.
Am I what I am even if I am nothing of the kind?

When I am alone, life is wanting another.
When you are here, your absence terrifies me.

The firecracker bursts before it leaves my hand.
Our meetings are brief; missing them sustains me.

The flag lost its colors but kept on waving.
Now that I am silent, you are ready to listen.

I shake the twigs out of my shoes.
The room I return to is not the room I leave.

10

The wanderer, his pockets stuffed with roubles,
can't change currencies at the wayside inn.

If I could walk to the end of one road
I would bury my shoes and vanish without a trace.

The telephone transmits the wordless spectre of voices.
The last time we touched was many months ago.

You want to give up the ship. I do too.
Only there is no dry land left to walk on.

I think of the tramp steamer that has been known
never to reach port with the same crew it departed with.

11

The moon is a white eyebrow. Faceless, bodiless,
it presses down on me so hard that I start to rise.

And now the broken body works tripletime
to the tune of the clicking heel and the crossing knee.

We used to grow old and die and be reborn: now only
gulches grow in the wasted spaces where no one fishes.

Time to go away, to stay here, to root in solitude
like desert plants that can thrive without water.

My shadow scythes the tall grass and lets it grow back again
instantly: this is the best way, to give and take life, and give it
    back again.

12

I have resigned my post and can't take
any more comfort from the clock or the calendar.

What we have lost will elude us like smoke in fog.
I have loved you enough, not past our satisfaction.

The farmer ploughs the rocky field; the horse eats
what is left of the ancient grass: he chews very slowly.

Someone scatters seeds around the ruined streets.
Confusion of tongues. Tilting of buildings.

What I take with me when I go
is what I will receive when I arrive.

FLYING

"We'll book you passage,
half fare rates,
there's no reason not to go,
there's nothing more to fear in the night,
radar takes care of everything."

Seatbelt sign flashing on and off
like a streetlight,
you never know when you can rest.
I ride with my belt on all the time,
as though it could save me,
as though it would not pull me down,
keep me strapped to the seat underwater,
my limp hair fluttering like eel grass,
like bait for barracuda.

Flying over water black water
I can hear the glue melting
even in the dark
over Las Vegas the plane drops half its cargo
over Los Angeles it picks up some stitches
over Arizona it is sucked into a pocket of air
the drunk's eyes go white
over Utah the engines growl
No Smoking No Smoking
it is summer it begins to snow
the mountains are higher than we are
the ceiling falls to greet the rising drunk
we are higher than the mountains
and below
the black fields of the midwest
we are dropping our landing gear over Chicago
just testing just testing
and I thought it was over
as the belly of the plane tilts
New York New York
steel grates on steel

engines heave and wheeze
I cannot see anything
hear anything
but the rumble of the jets
pulling at the sides
wearing down the wings
I feel myself
falling falling
bumped by hard pockets of air
eyes open eyes closed
me falling
ripped wings falling
bodies filing out of chutes like grain
someone I love is falling behind me
above me
she weighs less
though parts of us may join
with parts of others
when we hit dead bottom

It is like sleeping this falling.
I dream I am strapped, writhing,
into the dentist's chair.
As the gas muzzle is placed
over my nose and mouth
the whites of my eyes turn yellow.
I am losing air, losing air.
"Breathe only through your nose,
breathe only through your nose,"
runs through my head like a western song,
as I breathe only through my mouth,
only through my mouth,
as the chisel chops at the jagged tooth
that couldn't be pulled out or sawed off,
as though I deserved
an end like this.

I get ready to land on the hard water,
the endless blue slab
that will catch my fall,

and they will tell me
that fear is the cause of falling,
that I fell because I wanted to fall,
that the sharp thud,
the sudden dispersal of bodily parts,
is not the end.
The shock jolts my brain—
and for the first time
I see to the end of my mind—
a blue cave with porous walls
that go in and out.
There is a man at the end of the cave
imploring me to survive.
He is calm in a gray suit,
intense with gray hair:
there is light in his eyes
despite the many operations:
"Where do you want to take me," I ask,
"and why did you take so long to get here?"

"I came when you needed me the most," he says.
"If I'd been here before you would have waved me away."

TAKEN BY BROWN

Either there are no clouds
or they've all turned blue.
Is the floor still brown at the airport?
Was it ever brown?
It seems that everything
was a shade of brown
when I was there;
tan pants, amber jacket, auburn hair:
we slide down the scales of the colors;
paper, scissors, rock, palm, open palm:
down we go on the scales of pain;
we sink so fast
no gaff can reach our gills,
no gourmet can pickle our fins,
no souvenir shop can enamel our swords
and sell them to the bidder
with the largest lie.

The sun retreats for days at a time.
Mist hugs the ground like a wrestler.
The trees draw in their branches.
Beads of rain stream upwards.
The four white walls of the room
squeeze me out. Like a boat
made of weightless fibers
I drift through the screen.
Spiders chain their webs to the air,
and climb and climb.
The mountaintop blinks between cloudbanks
"straining after particles of light
in the midst of a great darkness . . ."
Goldenrod is a lantern past
the edge of an even darker wood.
I weave a crooked path
between the turnstiles of branches
jutting out of half dead trees,
leafy on top, pure stone on the bottom.
Thrashing through networks of webs
I stumble over a dead rat, large
as a rabbit, its four broken paws
propping up the sky.
Scanning every inch of its squat body
I feel no twinge of anything.
It's those nameless white animals on roadsides
that get to me: tire tread replacing the ear:
the car's grill creasing the belly.
And yet beyond this cell of trees I can still hear
to marvel at the delicate technology
of cows, the infant cries of sheep,
the almost human wail of porcupines.
The scene stays put: at night we hose it down
and in the morning it shines.

TOMORROW THEY WILL MOW THE CORNFIELD

(From an interview in TRELLIS 2, Winter 1974)

There is always more than one thing on our minds. We are always permeated with more than one feeling. I have a sense that a lot of poems exclude too much. Rather than moving up and down and around, following the sentences as they backtrack, get lost, dissolve, are reborn, a lot of poems construct a stance toward reality ("love poem," "pastoral," etc.). I think, maybe, that the only "type" of poem that does *not* automatically reduce the world to a scene, a setting, is the dramatic. It's no accident that much of Shakespeare's "poetry," in the plays, is *dialogue*; even in the soliloquies, which are what they are because the audience, the "other," is *there*.

***

I yearn for poems that include everything: the muted tones of late fall; love for another (for specific others); the news, Watergate and the irony of trying to continue "as usual" at such a time; the hunters with their guns and cameras and binoculars, tracking through the woods; the lovely deer that cannot feed themselves; the energy crisis; everyone berserk about waiting in line for gas; the simple existence of the natural world (not love of nature, but life in the country); the presence of trees, the fact of them, mud and sky and stars. Nothing anthropomorphic, nothing transcendental—simply presences, and the amount of work it takes, not to love someone but to relate to them for any length of time; the way in which conflicts do not end but are transformed; and how language itself, even used well, contains us as fully as our bodies, our physical selves, and how those limits are not dealt with, how the ramifications of that are manifest in the present historical nightmare. When a whole society is intent on destroying itself, how can an individual keep his sanity, and to what end, and in what context? Octavio Paz says: "There is no self, and within each one of us diverse voices are in conflict." But there is a self, and the presence of those diverse voices in conflict is its condition; the self constitutes itself out of them.

***

As I write, I am sitting in a converted barn. In Pennsylvania, in Amish country. When I look out the window, I do not see cars and tractors but horse and buggy. They seem to swish along the ground like streetsweepers. It is hard to connect the sound with the image. Actually, I cannot see the road from this window. It must be another window, in the house, the converted schoolhouse. From this window, there is only haze, hills, and humidity. I have not written a poem in a very long time.

I have been translating Pasternak's *My Sister—Life* and the Ukranian poet, Bohdan Antonych. I am trying to write some critical prose. I have to take my mind off myself and work on poems only when the impulse is there: to write what is truly essential, necessary. As it works out now, I have one writing stint each season. I didn't plan it that way; this is just how it turned out. Sometimes poems occur in between. These are gifts, but when I'm working steadily, it's hard not to think: "This is easy. I could do it anytime I wanted to." If I could change anything about the *way* my writing occurs, it would be my anxiety about the next cycle. It's hard for me to think of myself as just another part of nature. And tomorrow they will mow the cornfield.

***

One finds in the work of certain poets (Yeats, Vallejo, and Lowell come to mind) an almost perfect merging of the personal and the political (or the social and the individual), "the individual as an actor on the stage of history. . . ." They confront the world on its own terms, open themselves to the most raw and brutal of experiences, and yet maintain their life-energy and sense of humor. So much emotion and so little self pity. So complex and so immediate; so little stock poetry material.

***

I love babble: sound for the sake of sound, birdsong. The language of the cradle. I want to try to use such resources without becoming too "poetic." The universe radiates sound.

I would like for my poems to be as terrifying and funny, as bittersweet, as an Elizabethan drama. I would like for them to include all the emotional flux that life offers us, the ways in which pain, joy, sadness, ecstasy, depression, anger, all combine to form what is known as "personality." I want a form that is as immediate and intimate as a letter, that does not sacrifice intensity for intimacy.

NOTES ON "IN THE NEIGHBORING CELL"

I began to write "In the Neighboring Cell" as a kind of reply to a conversation I had with Nicanor Parra about "the future of poetry." Parra was saying that the whole idea of lyrical poetry was a holdover from the nineteenth century. Poetry now, he said, was to be found in graffiti, so he was actually copying down the graffiti he found and calling them "poems." Graffiti unconsciously expressed, or was the unconscious expression of, the conscience and the consciousness of the people. This is hardly a new idea, but Parra was adamant about its importance. I sympathized strongly with his ironic critique of the poet as a romantic figure, as a special person, and with his rejection of the "self" as an adequate and valid subject for our times. Neruda's early poetry, for example, is filled with negations of the self. But he could say, "I'm tired of being a man" because he was a man, all too human. He could negate himself because he had a self to negate. Parra's point of view needs to be considered within the context of his work, in which there are many splendid lyric and dramatic poems. Yet even if I had agreed, on an ideological level, Parra's ideas were, at that time, a dead end for me because I had barely begun to explore my own possibilities.

***

Poems are often written, consciously or unconsciously, as replies to other poems, as ways of saying, "this is beautiful, but your way won't do for me." In "In the Neighboring Cell" I wanted to have the city speak through me, and I wanted to speak through the city. In doing so, I wanted to avoid loading myself down with superfluous specifics, all the proper nouns that so many poets use as a way of validating their experience. In fact, the poem is a polemic against the whole idea of experience in "confessional poetry." There are many forms of graffiti in the poem, but all of them are imagined.

***

The city is bent on breaking down the sense of self, so the self in the poem becomes more and more of a spectator as the poem progresses (or regresses). In cities, we live amidst all the clutter of civilization and culture, without heat and hot water, with ceilings on the brink of collapse, with buildings themselves (tenements) ready to burst into flames (as ours did) like a forest fire at the end of a dry summer. Time is eaten up with the logistics of staying alive. How many people have any time or energy left for a personal life?

**

"In the Neighboring Cell" is intended to parody the autobiographical poem. I only say this because of the tendency today to psychologize everything, to forget that a writer writes out of his ambience. The negations are forged from necessity, from the necessity of adhering to his perceptions, not necessarily from self-hatred, sexual frustration, Oedipal agonies, not from any other necessarily "personal matter" that critics use to *explain* away the thrust of what the poem says.

So, the self in the poem becomes more and more anonymous, more and more of a generalized "citizen," an everyman, as he perceives the collapse of everything around him. The poem was my way of talking to the community whose sorrows I witnessed and participated in.

**

Mandelstam talks about the lust for rhyme of the old Italians, the expressions that flit across the face of the teller of tales as he talks excitedly; the act of speech distorts the face, destroys its calm. Then he goes on to ask how many pairs of sandals Aligheri wore out wandering on the goat paths of Italy (pointing at the relationship between the human gait and the rhythm of poetic utterance). I feel this is at the palpable core of the matter, of what poetry might be, of how it works, of how it automatically takes its place in the human community.

August, 1974

IN THE NEIGHBORING CELL

1

As I listen to the engine idling
I think of the stubborn horse
they gave me to ride as a child,
that horse who stopped to munch at every weedpatch,
whose reins I tugged
until my palms were gouted with blood,
while the other riders rode away;
of places I have long wanted
to cut out of my memory
but which waited like invisible ink
for the right light.

I cannot erase the chop of cities
stamped onto my mind,
cannot forget how my father must have felt
when my mother took me away
only to return fifteen years later
greedy to get to know him
while he fended me off
like an attacker.

Approaching the Holland Tunnel
in a taxi,
I huddled close to my grandfather's
broad shoulder,
and saw a man neatly sprawled
in the center of the street,
the broken white line
running right through him.

Drivers honked and honked,
pedestrians used his back
as a doormat,
the man flapped his right arm
like a wing,
pumping the blood out of his head

into a still pool
surrounding him.

2

It is raining from the ceiling
in the cellar.
The radiator steams the windows.
We can't see out, they can't see in.

When you touch the buzzer
shock touches you back.
The landlord wants to hang us
out on the line to die.

The landlord wants to build
white brick buildings
with elevators that rise
at the speed of light.

Tiles are popping underfoot.
Rising water beats
and beats
against the stairwell.

As the wave washes
over the second floor
a baby gurgles
for the last time.

3

This is where I live,
drowning under batches of inquiries,
lists for improvements
as necessary as water.

I dial numbers
as fast as my fingers will let me.
I talk to the officials of plaster,
the clerks of bricks,

the captain of the criminal squad,
and when the phone bill comes in
right on time,
and nothing has changed,

I start camping out in waiting rooms
thanking the pantsmaker
for making back pockets
big enough for books.

4

I note in the newspaper
that the news goes on around the clock,
that everything that happens is news—
so for today I would like to report
the failure of a lightbulb
to transcend its built-in time,
the tranquility of walls
in the absence of explosions,
the coherence of kisses
consisting of four lips,
the joys of hopping
a moving train,
and the lack of need
for any sentence
to end.

5

Max the butcher
was back in his shop today
sporting his old smile.

I was dead for a while, says Max,
but they brought me back.
Max the butcher

had a heart attack,
and I'm here
to buy meat.

6

The foam in the sink
is what's left of the clouds.
Perhaps they'll dry, leaving
a water buffalo in profile.

7

The steamshovel
disgorges another junkload
of priceless fossils:
a sack with more holes than burlap,
a briefcase strap with "L.Y."
intaglioed in gold,
a dry, nameless bone,
and some words
scrawled in red dayglo,
on a chunk of broken wall:
"Death has no future."

8

Under a white parasol
my mother reclines,
gesturing at the sun
to come closer.

My unborn brother
brings her an envelope.
The second he sees
my hard stare,

he loses sight
of his body.
He is invisible
to everyone now.

9

At times I am appalled
by the sounds of my own breathing,
and I fear that the body I touch
is not a body,
is nobody's body,
is the body of a body
and nothing else.

And when I think of what could be done
and consult scholarly articles,
I find that solutions abound,
and that I am the only one,
who doesn't know what to do!

Everyone but me knows what they're doing!
The horselover digging his spurs
into the horse's flanks
knows what he's doing,
just as the man with the crunching handshake
knows his own strength,
and the woman who hates sex
but finds her hand in your pants
is in control—
only I don't know what I'm doing.
Wherever I walk my body follows,
where my body walks walk I.
Surely it isn't the street that is cracking,
surely it isn't the tree whose trunk is bandaged,
surely the leaf growing out of your ear
should not distress you,
surely the way your hands resemble claws
should not send you to the dermatologist in desperation,
surely the fact that a mirror cannot find you
is no fault of yours,
surely your spine serves faithfully
as an axis to your body,
surely an axis never tires,
and when you walk through the rain
without getting wet,

surely it is the fault
of the shortness of your spine's memory.

Surely you know
that despite the trembling of your hands,
the liquid that spills
out of cups you cannot hold,
it is not a question of nerves,
for as you say,
you are calm, you are calm, you are calm.

10

Without negating the goals of renaissance men,
or blacking your shoesoles to keep them from looking worn,
or spending Sundays watching ballgames on television,
what claims can you lay to citizenry?

11

I began here,
learning how to tie
double knots
in shoestrings,
as though that could save me
from cold feet.

I shoveled dirt
from crate to crate,
tore out sections of sky
and filled them with roots.
Inside the crates
new lives were breeding.

12

Not the dusk filling the streets
like fog entering the syringe
or the click of heels on loose tiles
will tell me who I am.
I still sleep with a blanket over my head,

and keep my shadow tied to the hitching post,
and drag myself across the city
like a ladder missing all of its rungs.

13

The holes in the ceiling, the coffee
sticking to the saucer like a paste,
the dead lightbulbs,
were here before me,
but these bicarbonate of soda powered ships
were chugging through my veins
long before my memory
was as tangled as a shoelace
after the cat
has turned it into a toy.

Scanning the landscape
of curbs and corners,
tracking down a street
which is like a beast
made of claws and teeth,
I think of the danger
of looking too hard.

After I learn
to live with the streetlamps
as if they were trees,
and find no need
to resist the glacial shift
or the continental drift,
I will inspect the carpet
for signs of a future forest,
hang empty frames
on the flaking plaster walls,
sit on the fire escape
and watch the truck with the word
"Protein,"
blazoned on its roof,
and wonder

like any good citizen,
if I'm getting enough.

And when a man asks me
"which way to the nearest cannery?"
should I tell him
this is one vast cannery
or attempt with straight face
to give him the right directions
to the wrong place?

There are four tenants
left in the building.
The number of footsteps
far exceeds the number of feet.

From *THE HIGHEST SICKNESS*

In Spring the upholstery
of theater boxes was seized with trembling.
Poverty-stricken February
groaned, coughed blood,
and tiptoed off to whisper
into the ears of boxcars
about this and that,
railroad ties and tracks,
the thaw, and babbled on, of troops
foot-slogging home from the front.
You sleep, waiting for death,
but the narrator doesn't care.
In the ladles of thawed galoshes
the cloth lice will swallow the lie
tied to the truth without
ceasing to twitch their ears.

Although the dawn thistle
kept on chasing its shadow
and in the same motion
made the hour linger;
although, as before, the dirt road
dragged the wheels over soft white sand
and spun them onto harder ground
alongside signs and landmarks;
although the autumn sky was cloudy,
and the forest appeared distant,
and the twilight was cold and hazy;
anyway, it was all a forgery.
And the sleep of the stunned earth
was convulsive, like labor pains,
like death, like the silence
of cemeteries, like that unique quiet
that blankets the horizon,
shudders, and beats its brains
to remember: Hold on, prompt me,
what did I want to say?

Although, as before, the ceiling,
installed to support a new cell,
lugged the second story to the third
and dragged the fifth to the sixth
suggesting by this shift that everything
was as it used to be—
and anyway, it was all a forgery;
and through the network of waterpipes
rushed the hollow reverberation
of a dark age; the stench
of laurel and soybean,
smoldering in the flames of newspapers
even more indigestible than these lines,
rises into air like a pillar
as though muttering to itself: Hold on, prompt me,
what did I want to eat?

And crept like a famished tapeworm
from the second floor to the third,
and stole from the fifth to the sixth.
It gloried in callousness and regression,
declared tenderness illegal.
What could be done? All sound
drowned in the roar of torn skies.
The roar passed the railroad platform,
then vanished beyond the water tower
and drifted to the end of the forest,
where the hills broke out in rashes,
where snowdrifts
pumped through the pines,
and the blinded tracks itched
and rubbed against the blizzard.

And against the backdrop of blazing legends,
the idiot, the hero, the intellectual
burned in decrees and posters
for the glory of a dark force,
that carried them with a grin
around blind corners, if not
for heroic acts, then because two and two

won't add up to a hundred in a day.
And at the rear of blazing legends,
the idealist-intellectuals
wrote and printed posters
on the joys of their twilight.

Huddled in sheepskin, the serf
looked back at the darkening north
where snow gave all it had
to ward off death by twilight.
The railroad station glistened
like a pipe organ in mirrored ice,
and groaned with opened eyes.
And its wild beauty quarreled
with an empty Conservatory
shut down for holiday repairs.
The insidiously silent typhus
gripped our knees, and dreamt

and shuddered as he listened
and heard the stagnant gushing
of monotonous remorse.
The typhus knew all the gaps in the organ
and gathered dust in the seams
of the bellows' burlap shirts.
His well-tuned ears implored
the fog, the ice, and the puddles
splattered over the earth
to keep their silence out of the rain.

After BORIS PASTERNAK

43

All winter ice greased the windows.
The grape arbor was shriveled,
hunched over. Your tracks collapsed
as soon as they were formed.
Emptiness took on a coating
of dry worms evaporating at the bottom
of a drained pool. Headlights
bore through the skull of the dark
like lasers, and your eyes wanted only
to shut down. One listless afternoon
the twilight flickered down a lovely
and subtly undulating valley
you'd always skirted, now present
to your eye and your mind
and your rapid pulse racing
to meet a woman hours in advance
of the appointed time.
You forgot the future pulsing
like a tongue of light, and let
the rocks toss themselves
back onto the road like pieces
of crisp, fresh lettuce,
picked last summer by an old farmer
whose life was now confined
to a garden. The white line
was gone, but each car kept to its side
of the road of its own accord.
The radio pounded as usual
but the news flashed past
too fast to catch and for once
the windshield wipers
didn't give the rain a chance
to freeze into a sheet of metal.
You skid, and the dashboard littered
with plots for a torn future
throws the maps onto the seat beside you.
And the deer flash white tails

like roadsigns scattering droppings,
like a parody of buckshot into holes
left by your old footprints,
and now a retriever points
to what you have already found.

And when you pick it up it is not dead,
not even maimed. That red dog,
reared for hunting, hangs
his heavy head and his tail
flaps upwards in a blur of tails
like an upwards avalanche of wings
on a snowy canvas whitened
by flecks of salt crows stole
from the road but couldn't hold
in their beaks.

On good days the mud is only
ankle deep, as the waking mind
is attached to sleep. The sharp rocks
keep to the side of the road,
and the ax maintains its distance
from your toes. Not a year
that I have not lost my gloves
and spent the rest of the winter
in the cold. Except this year
when I borrowed my wife's spare pair
and never gave them back. I think
of domestic wilds, where it is lovely
merely to wake with her beside me
and have a clockful of minutes to spend.
The clock tracks us down
in the end, but until then
only runs as fast as we let it,
and I don't wear a watch.
I hear that research is being done
to find out what a steady diet
of doubt does to the heart.
My forehead is numb from too many
run-ins with walls.

Where is the guitar that will lead us
into a sequence of happy days—
complex, uncomplicated, intense,
serene and guiltless as a bad dream,
fed by an energy able to charge
dead lightbulbs through empathy,
being on our way flush with uncertainties,
digesting the daily toxic dose
of the news with ease. The news—
I had almost skirted it, and now I see
the tongues of broadcasters
wagging death between gleaming teeth.
Buds swell under the snow.
After a season of listlessness
the happy day bobs on the mudbank
like a raft for survivors.
What right have you to say that you're happy,
to talk about trees, to walk
around in public with your head on your neck?
Roots are scattered everywhere,
and they can't hear you.
The alphabet is deaf to your definitions,
and the earth is worth your life.
Birds twitter on target. Perhaps
they hear me hearing them.
The nagging issues of the day
attack your windshield like freezing rain,
but the windshield wipers
brush them aside like pawns,
and you are murderously happy,
rolling on the ground
right where you are now. Call it,
but you don't need another name for it.

There are no cattle in Abilene.
I expected cattle.
I thought they trafficked in cattle in Abilene.
And diners, I expected diners.
Abilene isn't even western anymore.
There are more foreign cars than cows.
The women are right out of Vogue.
I expected swimming holes and I got heated pools.
You could prowl the streets naked and never
Get arrested.
You could order coq au vin at any coffee shop
And get it, but fried chicken,
Never.
There is a local television station that runs
Old movies about Abilene all night.
No one falls asleep till dawn.
No one dreams.
I am out of it in my levis and Frye boots.
The streets are so smooth you could walk a lifetime away
And never wear the soles down.
One day they just stop moving. You gut them for your collage
And trade the label in for a pair
Made to disappear.
Everything in Abilene is replaceable.
There isn't much to talk about though
Except what's happening elsewhere.
The job is secondary.
I would have come back to Abilene anyway,
No matter what,
Eventually.
I was born there.
I spent my boyhood there.
I remember cattle. They once kicked up so much dust
Coming into town around nightfall
I could not see them but knew they were there,
In Abilene, then.
I earned my dimes shining shoes and I had a great view.

The women headed toward the wells with buckets.
Even the dust got watered, and the black flowers on their dresses.
Steam misted the windows of the Abilene Hotel.
Now the smoke of factories hides the factories.
The cattlemen never
Ran out of stories, or at least never told them
The same way twice.
I know. I was the kid. I listened. I was there.
Now everyone in town is all grown up.
Abilene, Abilene, Abilene, Abilene.
It could be an international city.
They should put up a monument and take down the town.

SIGNALS

[Chicago, 1958]

Threnodies of childhood:
hatch a nut; inhabit
a boxcar detached

from all the others
on a rusted track
where at erratic

intervals something
moves as on an empty
Sunday bent

over fragments
of a model airplane,
navigator grizzled, pilot

"new at the game,"
conscripted guide
out of his element. . . .

Threnodies of airplane glue,
first legal high,
sun razing the rust

off the trainyard,
glinting, sparking,
crossties green

with age and
hazardous with splinters.
You gazed back

at your electric trains:
the cattle stall on the ladder
to the cattle car,

buzz and jitter,
huddle, fall,
pile up, while

at the abattoir
padded stalls and false
backings keep those

perched in neighboring
tenements listening
for the final bellow.

Rubble out yet
another window
a jungle of rough

white stalk and hard
white rock
bleak, bleached,

like the high rises just
erected—conflagrations
of toilet paper

in the sink, porcelain
charred, blackening,
smokestack like an empty roll,

passport to juvenile
court in the poor box
you plunder under the nun's

habitual benign gaze,
and at school to sit
back of the girl

with the blonde braid
you tug for affection,
pledged to her white

and turquoise Scripto
and a Pez dispenser
that is never

empty when she
flicks it like a lighter
and lips the tiny pellet,

the rush when you kiss her
cheek in the elevator not yet
rooted in your cock,

her breasts stirring under
dresses of rustling chintz,
gawk, kid, at her first

shoots, snowdrops, startled
buds—and in back of you
the dark, refined, hard-edged

sophisticate Louisa
who taught you beauty's only
the beginning of terror.

You trembled at the sun
flooded open
boxcar door, mother's

tales of children being
locked in and frozen, hung
among sides of beef

in the freezer car.
You felt wired to die
upon transgression

and instead stole
lightbulbs from her cache
for your black comrades

convinced the empty sockets
were the source
of that heavy gray light.

THE MISSING DELFT   *After Vermeer*

1

Clouds
glide in estranged formations
over the bronze harbor.

The people on one shore
don't eye the people
on the other.

There are no
flags anywhere.

The city is belted
by a low wall
whose horseshoe buckle
is the only entrance.

Frozen bodies stand
poised at the belt hook.

Near to me
one woman wears
gull's wings
over her breasts
like a cowl.

If there is bread
in the gold and amber
straw basket she
balances on her wrist

it is not to be eaten.

2

Red roofs are yellow
this afternoon
and here it is always

afternoon.

The shadows of houses
fall into the river

a sturdy bridge
only the eyes can cross.

The living have no shadows
but the ground they stand on

is burnished ground.

3

Disparate items

glow

without the help
of windows.

Maps of the known
world on the walls and
globes on the desk
take the chosen

and they are all chosen

anywhere they want to go

instantly, without motion.

That is why no one
ever travels

or strings the lute
as long as there is light.

MATURITY

I have never seen
the ocean shallows

so full of leeches
or so much kelp

stranded in footprints.
I wade in.

The waves break—
too high to dive over,

too low to dive under.
All I can do

is lean into them
and keep walking.

I had no fear
of water as a boy.

I would mold my body
to the contours

of the water,
swim out, and drown

all noise from
shore warning

me not to go any farther. . . .
But it was never

water I feared:
It was air.

THE BLACK DOVE

1

That summer it was the castoff
hundred pounds of Idaho reds
sizzled in Crisco, salt
a mainline luxury, it was
a repetitious dry tickle in the throat
numb to water, our
armpits smelling of rotten
apples, your
belly swelling
with the child I'd planted in you,
however "impossibly."

2

On our second date,
dressed in black,
a martyr in the making,
you drove me straight
to your ex-boyfriend's grave. . . .

A draftee,
he'd put a bullet in his head
the night before
he was to report
for duty.

3

Simmering mornings I lined up
at the sawmill and,
as the wiry foreman, Sol,
picked us over like livestock
I cringed against the chalky wall
like a suspect—it had to be
some kind of privilege
to inhabit the inside of a hive

while planks collapsed and split
and saws broke their teeth on steel.
At least I was blessed by the salt
that crusted over my skin—
it kept the smell of my own
contracted sweat
away from my nose.

4

Numbed by then
to easy omens, spring's
most cherished inheritance,
a pet duckling no
fledgling anymore
waddled splashing
into a drainpipe at
yard's end never
to emerge. Sprawled
in muddy water, desperate
as a father to find him,
I aimed my head
through the opening
to no end,
thrust my arm in
up to the shoulder,
to the limit of my tendon's pull
to touch
nothing, to see
nothing, a
trickle of black ditchwater
oozed up my flashlight's
scalloped rim, that
and a pungent rot
gathered over how many years
I tried not to breathe.

5

It was this dream released me:
a thickset bald headhunter,

dull yellow snakes
tattooed on his forearms,
paddled a canoe up a slow
waterfall with the wrong
end of the oar, getting
nowhere in pursuit of me,
and as I plunged into the next
maelstrom to be spewn
into the next he never moved
while the current rippled
around him in silence,
and a black dove hovered
overhead like a hawk, treading
air, shedding
feather after feather,
and each one
took instantly to flight.

6

Now
in the tepid, portentous
summer of '76,
after witnessing
a Puerto Rican kid
wave a tiny plastic American flag
from the roof of a '58 Chevrolet
in full warpaint, in full
view of the Hudson as the tall ships pass
and their masts
drag the clouds upriver,
I come home,
rummage through old luggage,
and unearth a glossy blow-up
of you,
walking toward me and looking
down and away
on the path at the cliff's edge
that jutted over the glass city
like a gangplank,
and for the splinter of a moment—

rubbing my thumb over the dull, hard
edge of the photograph—I think
that the Amoco sign, deeply
submerged in the background, shaped
like a heart is still
blinking.

THE MAN IN THE ROOM *After Rembrandt*

That it could all come down
to a man in a room
empty but for

a ray of light
he resisted, seated
in a massive darkness

that was all shadow.
The walls were porous
but he never breathed.

He could have moved
into the light, been
for an instant

more visible than
the darkness threatening
to meld him with wood.

His skin cracked.
With all that
dust in the light

he must have known
that outside
people were

on their way,
their feet raised
the dust off the street,

bringing it
into the light
where it was lost.

THE BLOUSE

When your new gauze blouse,
your only gift to yourself in Paris,
came back from the hand laundry
with numerous minute furrows
where none were before,
your face was crossed
by such severe lines
it could have been
the block for a woodcut.

I tried to look at you
just so, so you would know I knew.
I tried to walk away
but my legs turned stiff like walnut.

A blouse of white gauze,
almost weightless, not quite transparent,
bought to flutter just off
your body and cling
more like an extension of the spirit
than an article of clothing.

And but for one errant iron
it might have been perfect.

FAMILY ROMANCE

Since her divorce, your younger sister
has picked the hours between midnight
and one in the morning to call and regale
us with horror stories but always

begins with someone else's pain, that of the
family carpenter who had lapsed into paralysis
of late, and no, nothing was new with her,
except for blacking out in the driveway

twice while lugging the family laundry to the car,
her three daughters sort of walking
all over her, and she has taken to falling
and hitting her head against walls since the accident,

you didn't know, she wasn't even driving
when the power brakes caught and the car
slipped out from their control hurling
her head into the windshield, twelve stitches

on both sides of the head, no worse
than her first concussion, didn't you know
her ex-husband used to punch her in the jaw
at regular intervals, and what

do you think she did when she found him
on the couch in her new apartment the first week
she was there, having left
explicit instructions with her daughters that he

was not to be let in, to see his face
hardened into a mask, his eyes
glazed over, his voice coming out with
a reasonable request, to take his three daughters

for a ride in the car, she ripped
that mask off his face and saw
the same face underneath, and nearly died,
and felt better than she could remember.

HOMECOMING

Another grim November,
no way out of that.
I stood under the same hard
thin layer of cloud
all day. It will stretch,
a friend said in Setauket,
to February. . . . Then I saw
the tarpaulin strung.

And endless field
matted down by weeks of rain.
The bruised earth:
it cringes under our footsteps.
We walk on.
I pick up mud from one spot
and drag it to another.
Stray clods of dirt harden.

The shadowed underbelly of a plane,
wind, rain, —
let the elements change.

The train windows, as always, are bleared,
like the voluminous cloud that shadows everyone,
now, as the season takes over,
forests razed, wood stacked,
flues opened,
the animals let in,
the rooms, as before, filling with stray things.
posters from exhibitions that have gone away hung on the walls,
whatever enters now, will stay.

How life lulls us—how all
is revealed to the sleepless!
Can you sunder your grief
on the foundations of bridges?

Where the smoky semaphore
chased night off the tracks:
where the bridge of the Apocalypse
rocks the sighs of stars,
where beams, ribs, rails, and ties
gather in a shrieking avalanche,

where jostled bodies grasp
hands, break embraces,
chant and repeat
a tireless refrain,

where the dipstick thrusts
benzine into faces
clinging like soot
on the ends of dead cigars. . . .

It's a burning tulip,
wild begonia fire,
inhaled by the crowd
through cupped palms.

The delicate pistils
burn as if ashamed,
every fifth one—engineer,
student, "intelligensia."

I am not one of them.
I was sent by God to torment
myself, my family, everyone
whom it's a sin to torment.

Near Kiev—sand
and splattered tea
stick to hot foreheads,
in fever—by social class.

Near Kiev—sand
in multitudes, like boiling water,
like the freshly washed trace
of a compress, like dropsy . . .

The tall pines can't dilute
this puffing, soot, and heat—
and now the storm juts out
of the forest like an ax!

But the woodcutter, where is he?
How long will all this last?
Which road leads to the depot?

Passengers clamber aboard,
the bell rings, the whistle hoots,
and the smoke spawns
a desert of its own.

Bazaars, illuminations
of night's finery, fog,
and out of day's weeds
noon and a saw lament.

You stretch your legs, hear
sobbing in the sheds—
hens and mattress springs
clucking, coupling in the sun.

I am not one of them.
I was sent by God to torment
myself, my family, everyone
whom it's a sin to torment.

Coffee, cigarettes, kefir.
It takes so little

to make me burst into tears—
some flies on a windowpane will do.

The pig in horseradish
sends tears down my napkin,
blurring my field of vision
like yawning rye.

For me to burst into tears
it takes only the odor
of tobacco from an editor's door,
or the heat to fall down,

or the click click of an abacus
amidst office gossip,
or desperate clouds to blow out
their brains on cucumbers,

or for high noon to strike
through the gauze of sleep,
or empty tables to rattle
at the call of cafes,

or the shadow of a raspberry bush
cooling my sweating forehead,
where greenhouses glimmer,
where the white body of a clinic stands.

I am not one of them.
I was sent by God to torment
myself, my family, everyone
whom it's a sin to torment.

Can it be that this midday moment
in a southern province
is not wet, barefoot, or hungry,
but racked with ecstasy?

Does that sulky, superfluous,
railroad hobo, that leech,

spy an angel's embroidery
on neighboring cherry trees?

Suddenly noon turns blue
as a sea of dots, and stoops
like a boneless shadow
hurled upon tired shirts.

Can it be that those willows—
chased away by railroad ties—
hurl themselves in a giddy spasm
to be embraced by a miracle?

Will they come back at night,
breathe essence from a wing
and start to play the housewife
over the strife of towels?

Will they spot the hazel's shadow
on a stone foundation,
or trace the spent day
in smoldering dusk?

Why make distress persist,
sifting through trivia?
The watchman switches our memory
and chases us off the tracks.

        After BORIS PASTERNAK

Beginning, not with our
arrival in the night
but with our first morning walk to the dock in the rain
 and the gull who, stunned out of sleep
deep in heaps of net
piled on net, rises drowsily, and angles off,
if this is possible,
without beating his wings,
which brings me back
to the rain
and only through the slight
prickling sound it leaves
on the thick
transparent plastic tarpaulin
can we hear it at all,
dazzled by the stalwart mortarless,
stone foundations in Maine
homes on the shoreline;
it is the ease with which they
receive the slashing
wave that imparts
loveliness to them.

My neighbor swears
the fireworks will be
worth seeing, and says
it's o.k. to stand
on the slippery dock
so long as you hold
onto the rail.

The fireworks do a fine
imitation of the
constellations,
ghost voices drift
over the water,
rippling under hulls,

scored rock,
incisions, wounds,
the boats that turn and turn
at anchor and spray shadows
everywhere,
turning, I see
tiers of houses
slanted on cliffs,
river, rivulet, and ditch,
luminous,
kids swinging sparklers in the dark
like censers,
lanterns hung
from the one beam
that will flood
the porch with light,
caracole
over two dwarf pines
rooted in shallow sand,
and bodies huddled
around a toy
cannon appear,
faintly present
in the red light under the flares.

Distraction sets in. Gossip
of lobstermen. I overhear them
talk of the warden, fall guy
for the decline in the numbers
they haul out of the deeps,
the abandoning of the quarry
doesn't count,
and they assail the warden
wonderfully,
"who sits on this
green schooner cut trim
as any canoe, the one
whose sails are never hoisted,
smoking cigars and drinking Martinis . . .
and when he caught me out there hauling

freezing my ass in the late November dark
I thought sure he'd revoke my license flat,
that sonofabitch, hell, it ain't fair,
there are guys out there without licenses,
raking out our traps in the dark
who don't care if they get caught—
but lobstering's the only thing I know."

AT THE ASIAN STAR ON THE EVE OF
ANOTHER DEPARTURE

Three cellos stacked against the window
of the Cuban-Chinese restaurant,
yet the lively air around them
doesn't connect to what I know
about cellists, the relentless hours
she sat erect over the dire strains
of Hindemith's "fifth"
(as she came to nickname it)
while I sought relief
from the continual
austere repetitions
she let take hold of the air
in kindred fifths of Spanish brandy,
and on stray weekends when
we camped in and buried the instrument
under weeks of laundry
and never wore more than bathrobes,
and never went out,
and ate randomly from tins,
and I told her I was AWOL,
and she told me she'd ditched her orchestra,
and offered another swig
from any of several bottles
containing the same thing claiming
there were no better
fifths anywhere,
put her index finger to my lips
and implored me in a voice
that dropped an octave
by Friday night
and whose timbre was more fierce,
serious, direct and deep
than it had ever been during the week
when we crossed paths
she used to say, "like ships in the night,"
with nothing ministering
to the loneliness we shared.

LOG

Journey to "Four Corners"

Ubiquity of the sign
"Bridge Freezes Before Road Surface."

America. Empty stadiums at dawn.
Beer mugs
soldered to men's fists
in Akron poolhalls.

109 miles of high tension wire
between here and Toledo.
Hills shaped like whales
and hills leveled for strip mining.
Hills like walled fortresses.
I must have forgotten the insignia
for "Mack" trucks was a bulldog
in convict's stripes.

Towns unlikely to appear in nightmares
race past "a mile a minute." Get
across the road woodchuck
I mutter to the creature
frozen in my path: downshift:
he goes back and the "Mack"
passes grazing my left elbow.
Over the Black River.

Whirlpools. Gulleys. Trucks.
I pass one sprawled like a toppled
elephant in the ditch
where the discarded shards of machines,
beehives of rust,
are scattered like relics.

Driving into the light side by side
puts the lust in us, our bodies
rustle under cool mottled motel sheets

and sleep comes any number of times.
The sky is constant at our departures.

Dawn rain. Crows
throw no shadow on the gray road
where the mashed collie lay.
Charcoal clouds swirl down.
Smoke spirals in thick
sulphurous braids.
Infernal air here,
ahead there is only
the outline of a man,
pipes and wires bent into this white,
animistic shape that multiplies
and stretches endlessly
as I drive into the light.

Searching for clearings
behind the eye,
silos multiply,
grain elevators rise
at the speed of light.

When our early, silent meditations
to the grave and airy
"Music for 18 Musicians"
dissipate in the bad hour, before noon,
I'm startled by the symmetry of cow and calves
in the trailer I dawdle behind
hungry. Crossing

another State Line
surrounded by Illinois cornfields
where I used to hide in childhood foxholes,
it all comes back—twenty years ago
the stalks were pliant, stiff,
rough green fibers, unwoven,
and winds that chafed my face
and dazed me. Now
harvesters groan to the edge,

shadows scatter over the fields
and freed from the glare I look up
relieved to see
cloud patches overhead
and wonder if they give
the only shade around here
in the raging, treeless air.

A vast meadow flared
outside our Best Western Motel.
And dusk held at the horizon's edge
long after stars had burst through.

Nebraska flatlands.
The absolute
division of the sky by one
darkening cloud: the rest
is an abyss of air. Time passes,
to all evidence, invisibly,
like the sky
that had no direction to go in
and hurled rain hard on our heads
and made us take refuge here,
in the desert air,
where the mountains are snow-capped
in summer.

Ubiquity of the sign
"D. H. Lawrence Shrine."
The roads in the hills outside
Taos are muddy, rutted,
and the wheels churn
the car to a standstill.

Feet deep in the clayey soil
we wade upward.
Lawrence's death certificates
hang on the wall like trophies.
I wondered what could appease
the spirits of the place

when a white cat,
standing sentinel on Frieda's headstone
upended an urn,
and all the ashes fell out
and scattered
and when I saw the cat again
its tail was entirely ashen.

Shapes in this light steady me.
Snow. Oval. Dome. Silo.
Shadows lengthen and stay.
But not for long.

Insistence on the literal:
    the shifting colors of the mesa,
tilt of the plains, scurrying

of tiny lizards, clickering
    of beetle shells, invisible
in the tall grass. In anger

at her reprisals. Noon:
    a mountain trail
that rings the canyon;

dwellings cut into the clefts
    visible through slats
in the sandstone reef—

cool hollow vaults that keep
    the same temperature
through the year: Low mortar corral,

oval fireplace under the square
    hole in the roof left open
for the sky—a rectangle of

light pinned to the wall—
    and still the fireplace
is charred and after

a thousand years the soot still
    comes off in my hands.
In light that keeps nothing back

from the sun the hill's thighs widen.
    Everything is used: pine pitch
stoppers the clay vessels,

the white cloud where sight
     breaks down hardens into snowy
mountain for the night, sky's

crystals, dry effervescences
     wild rose and greaseweed ground
to cure "mouth diseases,"

colloquies of crickets in the sage,
     tambourines in the scrub.
Design swarms through the mottled rock:

And the way this trail winds
     around the canyon, up is down,
in the heights, for the hawks

who trace arches in the air
     and never repeat
their firm trajectories. . . .

Gray haze of sulphur
     mars the horizon
no more or less

real now than row on row
     of signs announcing
what is in the town.

Now when I think of the chopped ice
      in the fishmen's window on Broadway & 100th St :
I think of it as sheep's wool, shorn,

and though I see the whole
      fish, the gray flounder, numb, frozen,
and the hacked slabs of salmon,

coral meat ringed by charred skin,
      it doesn't become the tawny
sandstone charred by dead fires, these

materials are never equivocal. Never,
      yet the shorn sheep and the grated
ice in the fishmen's window are one.

MIDSUMMER BLIND LUCK

Another house, another life,
a phone where we can call out and
no one can call in, leaving
the air rife with paradoxes
and voices on this party line:
what, then, does disconnected mean?
A path down to the sea through weeds,
thistles, fallen trees, and bridges
made of log or boards that collapse
upon the most cautious footstep
and you enter the welcoming
mud-suck. The thicket is this dense
because this house was uninhabited
for two years and nobody touched
it except squatters, whose mattress
springs have not abandoned the boat-
house. And I like swinging the scythe
through the tall stalks but a saw is
called for to make the passage down
to the sea passable—now it is
dangerous even if you're not on skis.
Found moose tracks in the mud
(or of another splay-footed
creature)—just two—meaning
it must have been the second half
of an interminable leap
I keep seeing repeat itself
across the path
like hummingbirds in the foxgloves
hovering still, waking the morning
with another morning.

TWO

BY CONTRARIES

BY CONTRARIES

> Without contraries there is no
> progression.
>
> *BLAKE*

1

I don't know how to begin because what I have to say does not go
naturally into language.

If children go to school, they carry satchels,
with brass latches, some bright bronze, some tarnished.

Rivers are far away, trees on both banks, branches motionless,
the water rippling, branches still. And the heavy leaves.

The wind is heavy in the heather. Swallows undulate and break.
Elephant seals loll, blond surfers in black wet suits dive.

My whole being is turned toward Poland. Not that I can avoid it.
The front page of the *Times*, the seven, the eleven o'clock news.

A room in a warm room. A room. A woman.
Not a clutch of spiders in the cornices.

*

In order to put up a new skyscraper on 96th and Broadway they
have to dig a hole. All day long steamshovels grind and gnash and
passersby stare. You could sell tickets. Nearly everyone who passes
stops and stares through the plywood fence. The holes are man-
sized. Yesterday I saw a man in rags, covered from head to toe
with colorful rag, and with an enormous strainer over his head,
and mauve rags over that, pause and waver there shuddering falling
backward on his heels as though the noise itself set off some
profound disturbance in his head, which I could not see; or was it
what he saw, coming down, coming down, being torn, and going
up; did he tremble because he knew what was happening? I know
only that he trembled, and that I did too. Finally, nerving myself,
I asked him what he felt. He expressed himself dimly, through a

mixture of animal and human sounds, grunts, whistles punctuated
by words:

"Why do you look at me
so strangely?
You would do well
to cloak yourself as I have
until the streets are safer.
The neighborhood
no longer knows itself
but better this
than an abandoned lot
of use to no one,
I mean, something
ought to fill this emptiness. . .
only not that."

Waking, I find myself gazing into the eyes of a Panamanian tree
frog, a head made of two eyes, like goggles, and a great bobbing
gulping throat: it is still dark and the flat voice on the radio
backed by furious clacking says—it is raining; or, it will rain today.
Or—snow: depending whether the predicted temperature of 33
holds or vacillates to the north.

I think of orioles, salamanders, bower birds, rivers, and thirst.

2

Driving over the Brooklyn Bridge the other night
during the momentary languorous dusk
that hovers before night falls and darkness hits,
it was as beautiful as anything:
the bricks warmed by the setting sun,
then the abrupt end,
the terror and quiet before the streetlights go on.

*
I think of the lights going on in all the houses
one by one, faces behind windows,
and imagine this village, where the lights go on

as darkness falls, the village Winslow Homer left out of "The Early
   Evening,"
where two young women in shawls and one fisherman
in something more seaworthy linger, gazing out to sea a last time

and everything can be read into what has not been said,

or seen,

like the silhouette wavering under the streetlight.

And then silence. The earth lost in the cosmos.

Beethoven's Quartet in B flat major, #13.

I do what I want. Whether I want to or not.
And so do you, you and you.

*

This senselessness persists and swells to canker redness
in the void, being alive.

And being born is all there is, according to the Albigensians.

Being here, elephant seals loll on some forgotten beach,
and she, in memory, is always holding something:
some twigs, seaweed, a cat, a child, myself,
through the cleft in the spiky yellow dune grass,
unbroken by the music of swallows.

3

The willful ego. A man has distance from himself, if he wills it so.
He has identity, purpose. His goal: to penetrate the gap between
the ultimate and the immediate. He thinks of Custer, Balzac via
Rodin and Rodin via Balzac, George Washington . . . with sudden
revulsion. He is not distracted by bracken and mire. He is not
distracted. He is what he sees:

The cathedrals burn.

They are not his concern.

All systems relative and fixed.

Systematic obliteration of the I/Thou.

A monster.

A crowded St. Petersburg street.
A face picked out of the crowd on the Avenue Napoleon.

Eyes wide, unshaven, ragged, he plunges through the rabble—
driven toward his mortal destiny.

*

How you have fallen
blind to the dawn star

to radiance until
it has been felled

and nations mown down
and nothing ploughed

and still planted in your heart
desire to rest

your ladder
at the horizon's edge

in heaven
no longer ascending

rung by rung
until there are none.

4

Blue leaves, red bark, spiky purple branches.
Tanks moving quietly through the streets.

"Hungary. Of course I remember Hungary."
"I have always been hungry."

"I mean the invasion . . ."
"I know. And when I say Hungary I mean hungry—

get that through your thick-skulled
fat-headed oblivious questioner's mask!"

*

You have not been singled out for special condemnation.
Nor have I. This is America, and while my thoughts
turn toward Poland and the worker's strike,
the Chief of State speaks of "acceptable levels of unemployment"
as, in Eisenstein's film, the Captain of the *Potemkin*
looks at a maggoty slab of beef and says
"Those are not maggots" with the utter calm
we attribute only to the ones
they never let past the asylum gate once they're in.
Benign when they are most evil.
Guiltless as children before they've been conceived.

*

Too much spinning.
Too many falls from branches
strung with glowering, and silence
and original despair—

strung with air,
the season's bare, haunted,
worn stare:
slate river, slate sky,

like a mask over a mask,
like the lines for unemployment
growing longer as the days
grow shorter.

5

Winter's coming in frazzled tints, yellow slickers, rain, not snow.
The jackhammers have not gone away since they began digging up
the street in early fall. Umbrellas have risen. Sunday the wind,
cutting corners on Riverside Drive, knocked down a woman and a
child. I offered them a hand when it hurled me against a building
as though I were about to be frisked and I wondered—*can this be*—
and—*what could I have done differently*—and I imagined the
woman and child starting to roll downhill like tumbleweed when
once again I intervened, and a voice, uttered this sentence, "La
distance immense que sépare le nécessaire et le bien"—then the
wind stopped and we all got up on our own, three dazed beings.
The sun was brutally bright in the cold air off the river. I asked her
what she'd said and she answered, with no discernible accent,
nothing. And I thought, what chance does the good or any moral
order have? Do the bricks soak up our presence in any way? What
are we here, equipped with wills, making decisions, choosing,
when at 4:25 you cross the Brooklyn Bridge and the city is
warmed by reddish light, dark clouds gather color and burn, it is
lovely, beyond thought, and then sudden, abrupt darkness—and
everything—the clouds, the river—the bridge itself—vanishes—until
the lights are lit. And all this happens *in one moment*.

6

In Zanussi's *Contract*,
the bride says no at the altar,
runs into the snow,
and the guests have the party without her.

The groom sets fire to his father's house
while the bride wanders through the frozen woods,
and a deer tips over the garbage cans,
and the prima donna clips one item from each of the guests,

and her daughter seduces an anonymous blond in the bathroom.
and they fuck in the tub—

*

I go to protest
the Polish State

at the Polish
Embassy, the first

day in rain and snow
the next in cold

cold sun
blazing conflagrations

on the East River
in tow with shouts

and tugboats,
whistles and smells.

The garbage rots
in the garbage, we

rage. Police
gather on horseback

in blinding
yellow oilskins.

Rats tunnel through rods
of·black plastic bags

like the Beaubourg
in Paris

and I wonder
what Oldenburg

who so loves the giant floats
hovering over the Thanksgiving

Day Parade would think
of this

natural, unnatural
construction.

*

It's the urban glare but it can get to you
anywhere—hear the rat grind its teeth

even now in Jerusalem, how fiercely
the toothless crone protests that her new

shipment of wooden bookcases
and dislocated drawers are made

of "real wood, not pine,"
the quaver in her voice,

pain coming through as pain,
its message being one. Only hope intrudes.

7

Beethoven's late quartet #13. Talk about gravity. The first move-
ment is the body. The second movement is the spirit—and it flies
—without hesitation—hinged to the invisible—giddily—verging on
laughter—more spirit in the sound than any religion has conceived
of—it is extant—this spirit—and translated by the instruments
(though they and the players have trouble keeping pace)—the
gravity seems more innate to Beethoven than the laughter but the
latter is alive in this one—

Only among his friends at the tavern did Beethoven experience a
kind of transcendental *distraction*. Everyone spoke at once, so
that Beethoven, who had become deaf over time and had known
well the laughter of the table, never felt left out.

*

My grandfather became blind gradually over the last ten years of his life. At the point where he could see only the last blurs in the visible world he took me to a silent movie: *The Gold Rush*. Why? Because I'd never seen Charlie Chaplin. (And the theater was right across the street. . . .) We entered when he was about to feast on his shoe and laughter rose in bursts from different parts of the room and wafted around. My grandfather started to laugh before we sat down and kept turning toward me to see if I was laughing. I was laughing. I was laughing and taking deep breaths. And I felt his blindness for the first time, felt it as though it were music. Not that he was feigning pleasure. Not that it was absurd that he should laugh at something he couldn't see. It was the incongruity that made me register his blindness for the first time, and feel it as though it were mine. And the thought of the suffering he'd endured was as intolerable to me then as the fact of his death was to me later. Intolerable. But he didn't see it that way and maybe that's what happens to the mind over time. Same as what happens to the body. In another way. Same as the tension between the flesh, body, worldly self, and the spirit in Beethoven's quartet.

8

Boston has three feet of snow. Why doesn't New York have snow? It has squalid, flesh-colored rain instead.

She said, I want to meet you in a neutral place.
Anywhere, I replied, anywhere.

She said, "The more you talk the less it means."
How this mistrust of language becomes a contagion.

"With you it's always I, I, I, I, I, I, I. . . ."
And silenced my reply.

"People are not collectibles," I told her.
"What are they then?" she answered.

"People disappear every day," she said.
Every time they leave the room.

9

Morbid it may be
and maybe not

unwittingly. Who
among us knows

the right direction
when all the arrows point

to known roads, and when
in the kitchen, time

dissolves in the riot of vegetables
edging over everything

exfoliating still
miraculously

out of the ground
like someone I saw months

or years ago
on Lispenard Street

walking, and not moving
in the same instant

in continuous motion,
and I see her now·

through this haze
mesmerized

by the slowness of her gait,
her refusal to stop or to go anywhere,

her sense of being herself
forever

in the same instant
I have lost. . . .

Vision unredeemed
pains the senses.

So the teeth lock
and the hand becomes fist

and the chest—the chest tightens
not to ingest—emptiness

because there is,
between catastrophes,

being in what is,
and this,

the psalmist sings
is happiness.

10

It's that time in the century to dream
of heaven again, shuck off all impediments
to transcendence and sense and join in.
The ring is already forming,
orotund and mute.

In the crowded, dark domed room, the light
pouring from four open exits burns your eyes,
the doors swing loose on their hinges
and you fear that if you enter
you will disappear.

Don't enter this room!
No one's in there
anymore to answer.

Death, breath,
one foot, other foot,
the last step

no closer to home.
Don't trust anyone
who has nothing to hide.

*

It can't be true, what I just saw walking uptown. It staggers all
sense. Two black policemen, drawing guns, entering an SRO—
slowly. A teenager opening the door for them and backing into
the street to look upwards after they disappear, and no I don't
wait around to see what happens—BLAM—and no this is not a
movie—BLAM BLAM.

Fog on the river hovering over the stubborn trees and spiky
branches: an idyllic hell but still a hell pervaded by the desire to
endure. Strange gray in the air alive with dust. What is it I see?
Rivers dividing the city. Row on row of empty storefronts make
me remember all the errands I have forgotten to run and what we
need to weather another winter. More light.

> What we call real estate—the solid
> ground to build a house on—is the
> broad foundation on which nearly
> all the guilt of this world rests.
>
> *HAWTHORNE*

11 / *Waiting Out the End of Winter*

I think of Maine. The slightest degree
of peace. The merest morsel. Infinitely smaller
and harder than a crumb. Madelaine with her wand
making each constellation appear, giving design
to all that glittering. And the body's victory.
Or defeat if fog lasts more than three days
and turns us invisible in the rooms we once lived in,
now stumble through, yelling warnings and hellos
like ghost ships in fog covering one island,
another, and another, until this white wall grows
to the edge of where we are, rising farther
than we could ever hope to see.
I have lost myself again and I forgot
where I began. Peace. Stillness.
Wavering ears in the grass. The telephone dis-
membered on the lawn for the children of lobstermen.
Gray green shimmer of water over stone.
I remember what it is to be human:
breath before death. After the fog lifts
I walk down the steep hill to Naskeag Point
and watch the tide back up over humped,
kelp-bearded, barnacle-crusted rocks,
and while waiting for the boats to come in
fix my eyes on an oarless skiff
that looks like it was made to sink,
or stay on shore to remind strangers
who have no trouble getting lost and are grateful
for an abiding presence and every time I return
the pines on the nearest island move
a little closer. Nothing stays.
Nothing goes away. Not the wind

even though the treetops are utterly still.
Not the islands even when fogbound.
Nothing goes away. And nothing stays.
A good day to start out on a journey.

12 | *Escape*

Drumroll of days.

Max Roach's spirit in the deserted
gazebo, framed by arches.

Women and cellos.

"People have a lot of trouble with
feelings," she said.

"I have so many patients who can't
acknowledge anger, or loss. . . ."

*

Cloudless, the crowd forsakes its trenchcoats.
They pile up on the ramparts of the forgotten winter.

No traces—only the residue of smells in the sopping
mat of leaves on the cold stone floor.

Running the gravel grazed path, winding
in an unending circle.

"This is the end," she said.

"It depends on what you mean by a scandal."

*

"Cut my hair green," he said,
sinking into the Unisex chair.

Cold sun on the windows.
No leaves, the trees

plastered with posters
from foreign countries

where sunburned bodies frolicked
in the waves.

His friend was en route to St. Thomas,
no, St. Croix, St. John,

somewhere, he was sure,
in the Virgin Islands,

and he needed to get away,
to escape New York,

that's why the green hair, the. . . .

*

The man ahead of me is lugging a suitcase. I quicken my pace,
wanting to ask him if he heard gunshots too when he stops, drops
his suitcase, flicks open the latch, submerges his hands, withdraws
them wearing boxing gloves, turns toward a dim, lime-colored
streetlamp, and starts throwing punches, jabbing, dancing around
this inanimate object, muttering ugh, come on, yeah, got yah,
missed me—and I decide not to ask him if he heard anything and
continue moving: past abandoned baseball diamonds, fish frozen
at the waterline, rocks imprinted with feathers and the filaments
surrounding the quills of other species of birds, the ice jostling and
swirling carried along by the river's current, growing smaller with
every step I take in this, or any, direction, with every passing
moment—whether you or I are there to witness its dissolution or
not.

The ice hardens imperceptibly and palpably dissolves and breaks
apart. I remember thinking, seven years ago, in sickness, the year
we returned to the city: this winter will not end. And here I am,

aware of my earlier error that makes me shun absolutes, no
matter how edged, or whetted with irony.

After all, there is the world. . . .
The *it* of it, streets welling with slush
and deserts cracking from the absence of water,
the glint of waves and hubcaps, cosmos and dunghill,
phobias, isms, plague sore souls lost,
$, items, borderlines, questions containing answers—
mud, salt crystals, Robert Smithson
living to see the Spiral Jetty,
dying before it went underwater,
embalmed in photographs, tacked to feverous museum walls.

These are small amusements. In a harsh winter.

13 / *Peripheral Vision*

I am writing from a city where winter has gone on too long and
even the lizards and iguanas headed south after the last blizzard.
The Whitehall Hotel is empty. The black man in the wheelchair
who wore sunglasses through the year and sat under the ragged
awning in the rain, or sat beside the awning in the sun, the center
of activity, is gone; and studio apartments are going for $700 a
month in the yet unrenovated, mice-strewn, rat-infested hovel!
Soon the "new gentry" will occupy the old rooms of the unem-
ployed.

The only thing new around here, other than conspicuous absences,
is construction. I scan the Real Estate section of the *Sunday Times*
with the "real" in the lower case and the emphasis on Estate, and
think of owning something that is not merely "For Sale."

Further traces of dereliction. Walking uptown through Riverside
Park—between parapets—I hear gunshots: one, two—no more. I
think—pay attention. And test the limits of my peripheral vision.

Nothing, no one. Helicopters coming in awfully low, grazing the
tops of buildings where people are walking their dogs on the roofs.
Tugboats leaving thick wakes, like waves caught in the churn, in

the density of stop-time. Gulls, not pigeons, wheel and cry—
through the pinks and grays of the factories—diving in and out of
the trees.

14 / *The Punch*

To take advantage of the January thaw, I walk
uptown to savor the grapefruits and green
peppers in the winter light, then, returning, turn
the corner to see the aftermath of a slap,
a lover's quarrel perhaps, no, nearing the red-
headed woman who is crying,
and three, four, five, or six
gathering bystanders,
it's clear that wasn't the case.
"I wasn't doing anything," she says
between her tears and the fiercely red
right side of her face,
"she just came up to me and hit me."
"Who her, that one?"—the woman, girl?
strutting down the block and as we stare
at her back turning on her heel as if
she overheard.

The redhead speaks with an Israeli accent,
English is definitely not her first language, and
it's not clear whether she's more hurt or shocked
but no one knows what to do.
One assumes so much.
That the two were walking toward each other
rather than parallel,
that the girl stepped abruptly into the woman's path,
grabbed her left arm, shouted at her,
and cracked her across the face with the palm
of her right hand,
that the redheaded woman was lost
in her own thoughts when this other person
surprised her.

I find it impossible to assume that they were walking
toward each other, like gunfighters, from one end

of the street to the other, difficult to believe
even that the redhead sensed danger
more than seconds before the girl accosted her,
inflamed by her red hair and pale skin,
and yet so much of what I reconstruct
has to do with how they acted
during and after the actual blow,
the girl strutting, jaunty,
the woman slow to react. . . .

My sense now of what I saw is that it wasn't a slap
but a punch and that it was random,
transcendentally stupid, but then
why should asteroids be confined to outer space?
The deception lies in the human form.
In the sunlight, doled out one morning.

15 / *Orphanos*

I had the vague edge of a tune on my lips and that was all. I can't
remember if it had a name or if I made it up out of some longing
for quiet on this night when sirens are unending. I could live with-
out the sirens, drills, the endless digging in the streets where man-
holes grow wider by the day, and the garbage trucks arrive and
begin to grind before morning, and I would like to see the stars
again. That's all very well, she says. I can hear her breath in the
long night without sleep. It doesn't help the next day, the memory
of her there, but it does give a blissful edge to insomnia and when-
ever I whisper Are you awake, she always answers Yes and then
we both lapse back into silence, hoping, in most cases, to sleep.
No longer to remain alone. No longer to pretend I do not fear
being abandoned.

16 / *Generation*

Entering the park, twelve women on horseback,
not counting the instructor
who appears when they have passed.

Absolute stillness.
Soft echoes of footfall.
Light curling, coiling in the branches.

The reservoir is covered
with a thousand snowy seagulls
and now one hovers grayly at eye level,
stops. Absolutely still.

No sound of drills.
Baby carriages in place of horses.
Radiant mothers at the helm.

Light crossing the branches,
hanging suspended in the slow
time of late afternoon.

17 / *Brooklyn Bridge Centennial*

The city is paved with people. The fireworks shoot up, hang in the
air like tendrils, and wiggle away like sperm, each flare mounting
higher and higher—if only they could remain in the air at their
most exquisite, reticulate point, rather than fall and die, a config-
uration of interlacing lights could stay beside the bridge forever
like a tree.

And to think that half of the bridge still has its roots struck in
sand.

Afterwards we walk through the neighborhood where we used to
live, past all of the converted warehouses, through a futuristic
housing project out on the pier where the PEKING is docked but
the crowd, on its way out, begins to rumble and grind and I begin
to fear a stampede. Then the fog comes and washes away the
smoke. The bridge is barely visible in the haze until they turn the
lights on—after the fireworks are over—and I think the planet they
sighted in the next galaxy has landed.

It had landed. Long ago. I think if I stepped aboard the PEKING
I might end up in China.

"Why do they always portray the people as a faceless mass?" I ask a photographer who has just returned from a six week journey by train through China. "That's what they look like," she replies. "Everywhere you go everyone looks the same. It's a visual thing."

What you see is not what is. There is no way, only one way, to oust a certain poverty of the spirit. And not in so many words.

18 / Duress

My mistake was in thinking I should not
be unruly, feel one way this minute

and another way the next—
without exception.

I didn't even understand what I had done
to myself, to you, and others

who cared and were indifferent,
or that being-in-sight

and out-of-mind were not
contradictory states.

I didn't understand,
and do not dissimulate

underneath the green
surface of this confession, this

owning up to what I didn't understand then
and do now, now!—

while the elements themselves
conspire to mock discovery

unblemished, like the rain.
I meant, simply, to say:

it is raining. It was
predicted but did not fall

until now. Or shortly before
I looked up from the old wall

I was tearing down piece by piece
with this shiny new crowbar

that takes on a strange beauty
with each new dent.

What made me think
there would be less pain,

less certainty,
less violent change

from second to second
when there never was?

I' th' commonwealth I would by
contraries
Execute all things.

GONZALO, THE TEMPEST

19

I am dazed by the sun coming out for the first time in days. February is a rum month here. Emerging from underground, a strange quality of absence pervades the crowded streets, the empty shops and theaters. Soaked to the bone in the rain I take refuge under an awning on lower Broadway wondering *what feels so strange*. It's been dark all day long, the electric lights are ringed by a faint haze in the mire, the pitch dark day—the yellow glow of taxis stands out, colors leaping, gyrating, as people's faces lean toward the invisible, the murk, that waits to swallow them bone by bone. Bodies, dripping with pitch, drag through the mire, clutching briefcases and shopping bags—the last to go. Stepping on a pair of sunglasses I catch my breath and hear the glass and plastic crack underfoot; kneeling to gather the remains I find, stuck to the pavement, a black calf-skin wallet. What to do? I look around—same parade in the darkening haze, disappearing through doorways, negotiating revolving doors without getting caught in the mechanism. I peel it open, slip my fingers into the tightly packed side pocket, feel plastic soft and hard, *credit cards, photographs*, and tug the hard, preferring the name over the face . . . *Visa* . . . first name . . . Lulu . . . I shove it back, withdraw the soft plastic packet containing photographs of skyscrapers only, glittering crome and glass,—myriad eyes,—in Anywhere, U.S.A.

20 / *Darkroom*

That's why the ragged clouds wept shamlessly
all morning over thistles and steeples,
and a woman bought an avocado
outdoors at a green grocer and said
no I don't need a bag, and the vegetable man,
who spoke almost no English other than yes and no
and the name of everything he sold,
tried to pull it out of her hand, smiling,
shaking the brown paper bag in front of her eyes

until she cried and backed into the street
only to stumble over the body of a black man
who'd been literally broken, cracked, bone by bone,
hit by a delivery van the size of a house,
his face dazed, eyes red,
and the woman, already in tears,
now numbed by the thought
that this man who'd been hit
while she was bickering and being stubborn
was soaking up every ounce of pain
in his brain, and she began to hear
a decided thud, and thought
that must be why I've been so upset today. . . .

21

Nobody in the other room. And when he shows up at the construction site they hand him a pick and tell him to dig. When the old, dead cement is broken down he asks for a shovel. No shovels given out without wheelbarrows. He looks up at the rust colored skyscraper, already brushed by clouds, clouds in the windows before it's been completed. The wheelbarrows, lined up in a row in front of the ditch, are choked with rust colored water from last night's rainstorm when lightning reverberated in his inner ear. Terror. The blankness of matter. Ashes come down from the sky, boiling the sea. Men are islands and they burn in that instant when a leaf turns and a single flame comes leaping out of the burning forest. The grid of rain and trees and branches on the mountain is terribly logical, like systems, like madness. When I got there they were burning leaves in the garden. No flames, only a slow, smoldering fire. They were burning furniture. . . .

22 / *Making Belief*

It doesn't take Kaspar Hauser
to tell us what lies
underneath the grass
and flowers of the lie.

The body could have
moldered in the sump forever
had no one found it
out walking in search

of nothing—other than a way—
into the next labyrinth.
No word is congruent with despair.
Some things only make sense when whispered.

The trees know this.
The wind soughing in the trees knows this.
The spring peepers, growing in number by the hour, know it.
I, when I am myself, know it.

The sighs and groans I hear,
the aimless gestures, the forgotten traces,
the moans in the hinges of doors know it,
and so do the mudcaked tires of my old, worn, Rudge bicycle.

Things know it better than men do.
The snap and click of latches on plastic briefcases
break the rhythm of the actual,
the fact of it, entirely.

23 / *Deserted Springs*

In the first hours of spring the city flocks to the parapets over-
looking the river. The people gaze out, smiling, grateful for the
warmth and light, the quiet. The traffic pours into the river, flows
up, then down, vanishing. My eyes circle the roots at the base of
a tree. It is alive, I think, I am alive. Everyone here now is alive. It
is not nothing to feel what you think you know, or even worse,
take for granted.

I have seen the moon rise over the rooftops two nights in a row,
the full moon snagged between spires—dead center—over the clock
that tells no time. I saw it between the eyes and passed on in
silence, dying my own death, bewildered, lost in the lost city,
wondering why I returned, as if being born here were not enough.

As if I had not melted already when I kissed her first in the sand-box, and tasted her cheeks against my cold lips.

Dogs follow a woman to the river's edge. She is wearing a red letterman's jacket. The air is warm, the wind cool.

The dogs howl riverward.

Absence. Quicksilver. Rage flickering in the veins.
An electric current strung through the known world.

Yet I left everyone leaning over the parapets, backs to the city, hovering, then tossed into the vat and locked away.

Shadows take everyone.

Get that guy, the shadows commanded.

Dark and cold. Remembering how, half my life ago, I found myself alone in the desert, abandoned, drunk. Motorcycle in the ditch, spokes glittering. A cactus spinning. The Milky Way wheeling. Laughter in the dead gulleys.

A beer bottle tumbles, echoing, down a ravine.

I am drunk, stumbling over my own footsteps.

Something edges toward me with an inhuman grin.

I am not only here to tell the story,
I am here, telling the story:

Once . . .

24 / *The Pyre*

The rain dissolves everything human,
the wood swells, the rust on hinges washes away,
the cat drops the dead field mouse on the back step
under the eaves where the bat sleeps. . . .

Another summer solstice celebration in Quebec—
thousands will gather in the hillsides
around bonfires
while I drag another log in
heave it into the fireplace,
gather sticks and bark for kindling
and, rolling up pages of the *Times*,
come across the list of those newly dead,
kneel, light the fire, and go for more logs.

No longer to ponder the morbid denials,
I will mourn, break down the sentimental,
human distinction of age.
Let the fire rage.
Let these ashes stand for life—
raw, unkempt . . .

The pain, then, of numbness, I sing, now, in the drear.
I started to sing last night at low tide,
and for the first time in a long time heard my own voice.
I lulled the clear, cool air
with the names of what I could touch—
tree, rock, shell,—smell—
the sea,—and see—
sky, blue, crow, black, gull, white,
island, tidepool, kelp—
and hoped no one would overhear.

25

These bare islands broken by no inhuman gaze,
where lichen hangs down from the fir trees
and nomads wait for low tide
to rip mussels from kelp entanglements,
blood draining out of the veins,
the icy water pulsing, the heat delirious and the sun
on your forehead long after it goes down,
the blood flooding back, the constellations rearing
for the northern lights to fling green beacons
fanning edge to edge of the sky like a spiderweb. . . .
And no light on in any house I can see

from the road, and no one around.
And it is possible to think.
To have a thought
as the elements themselves
wage war on your nerves.

26 / *Solidarity Reconsidered*

> "I can take the crisis
> just spare me the crap."
> *A Polish Punk rock group.*

Sunken cities, smoldering bays,
        intrusions of sunlight,
a map of Poland with the factory
        at Gdansk circled in red,

the news in slow dissolve,
        arrests, internments,
Jaruzelski: "We are moving toward normalization."
        Conveniences deny

the nightmare I wake to,
        at the circle's center,
inhumanly molting, leaving
        a trail of shed snake skin

on the single bed's cold sheets,
        or on the paths that wind
through thickets toward the city
        or swerve in the other

direction—toward the river. Paths!
        To wander down now without
protest from the cells!
        Rhythms the body reveals,

and the day and the night,
        and the shy blackbird sideways
on a haunted limb. And so
        in a few days, a few

hours, eternity comes and goes
and no one sees it:
it sees you and seizes you
and stands revealed.

27 | *Threshold*

I always end up walking down to the sea
as though it were the beginning or the end
of something other than elapsed time,
marked by the creaking of screen doors,
rusty gates, and water.
And the pebbles, shells, and scales are utterly still.
At the beginning of another century.

THREE

Men are miserable by necessity, yet determined to think themselves miserable by accident.

Giacomo Leopardi

You receive a different impression from a building under construction where the details are not yet shown, than from the same building when it has received its full complement of ornamentation and finish. It is the same with ruins, which appear all the more impressive because of the missing portions; their details are worn away or defaced and, as with buildings under construction, you see only rudiments and vague suggestions of mouldings and ornamentation.

Delacroix

THE TARASC

Mythical child-eater
made of papier mâché
I discovered in a garage
in Tarascon.

A huge toothy
red and green carnivore
in the dark of the garage,
a shadow of

the fabulous monster
on medieval woodcuts
who leads the parade
dripping children's entrails.

Photographs
of the Tarasc.
His frozen gaze.
Terrible in stillness.

The heat of Provence
flowing through
the shadowless
street in Tarascon.

The clicking of shutters
that accompanies
this century
as it fades.

LONG SHOT CLOSE UP

"Tragedy is close-up, comedy, long-shot. In *Contempt*
I tried to make a tragedy in long-shot."

Godard

1

This way come the ravages of the snow,
singed by the heat

behind every window.
The *where you are going*

becomes surviving the getting there.
I dream of harbors, of the harbor

in Marseille, the heat of that afternoon
when they disappeared and we melted

on the steep, shadowless streets, killing time. . . .
I remember the boats moored in the harbor,

their black flags lowered to half mast.
Or is the flapping of sails

in the windless air
closer to what was.

Or what really happened.

2

The city looks other planetary in the fog,
the lights in the windows dim,

the sky as gray as the plane
passing through with its lights on,

as gray as the cloud swallowing the plane
casting a darker shadow

which stays where it falls on the Hudson
like a meteor in a desert,

like a solitary heaven chained to a pinball machine,
pressing the flippers,

sending a metal ball
clacking back among the plastic planets.

3

And to experience the pure joy
of being alone in a room,

the brilliant winter light pouring in,
unforgotten, gone,

only known, intuited, through
another's bones

arranged around your skeleton.

1

The classical starkness of the trees in the park, or:
a winter's tale of stark trees and fur
and neighborhood gossip comes down to murder
and several fires so that there are fewer and fewer
buildings to burn. The illusion of life
in the scaffolding. Not like the day last summer
when we lay like lizards on the rocks off Naskeag,
the day you got lost on our driveway. . . .
Wintering kills any delusion that life
lies in the sunlight, behind the next bush,
where a woman walks in a cotton skirt
that clings to her thighs in the heat. . . .

2

"Take a moment." Or do you need *time*.
To rid yourself of the malaise of "good intentions."
Trees   laundries   cancellations
        hesitations   depressions—
a farce that enables us to live. . . .
She dreamt her doctor's office had been
converted into a stable in the rain.
And these fires stacked along Broadway
like lumber on a barge are all Monday trees.
She wrote from Italy, "Suddenly I thought the world
was made of wood, the habitable world . . ."

3

Days out of time you did not seek.
Fences appeared, with gardens behind them,
lovely women in thin cotton dresses, sandals,
with bare shoulders, hesitated in the light
to look at gingko leaves on trees
or yuccas in the windows of florists.
And just to touch her skin I feel
the heat at the center.

A thaw in the city has its own violence:
suddenly the air smells of everything it has inhaled,
smoke and cement as much as grass and bark,
gasoline and tar as much as leaves and skin.

I saw what was there and it was not what I saw—
naked men and women frightened
showing no fear
alone together and in the end alone
even when together no one there.
Humid air. Some hopeful skulls.
A he skull and a she skull
split by a live skeleton
standing over the graves of the living.

Sight made visible at last!

This Saint Francis in the desert
grubbing blindly for the one skull
in a mosaic of bones.

One of the seven deadly sins
is missing from the deck.

Vines crawl the spires above "The Famous SOUP BURG"
across the street from the Whitney Museum
where I order a rare hamburger and water and they
hold the water
while I die of thirst.

And think of Fischl's painting where a boy
leans forward on the end table,
his eyes on the woman who lies
back in bed with the sole of her foot
propped on her calf,
exploring her vulva with her fingers,
palm down on pubic mound,
while the boy, avid, lustful, dying,
his hand thrust into her purse,
leans further and further forward until he falls—
the two of them forever unappeased. . . .

Dying of thirst,
I summon the courage to ask again for water.

Water.

No limit to the unending present.

It thunders for an hour before the first rain falls.

And men and women
are emerging from taxis,
groomed and slick
even in the downpour.

Beyond weather.

Unlike the rest of us
who feel our bones being
washed away underground,
the rest of us—

on subways, buses, or on foot,
sweaty, mangy and mangled,
stained by the beautiful
insistence of the hour.

A man, a woman, a garden.
The necks of horses
stretching out, flattening,
at the finish line.
A woman catching her breath
after the train
has left its spray
of smoke and steam,
vapor over the tracks,
obscuring the clematis
in the garden I cannot see
on the other side. . . .
The spaniel puppy
sleeps in her lap, which is why
she can't turn the pages of her book,
and looks up as if to say,
"If I move my hands I'll wake the puppy,
and the young girl,
already riveted
to the trailing smoke,
holding on by holding on
to the bars, will cry!
And all I have to do is turn the page. . . ."

Or the races at Longchamps
where the horses end up
right between your eyes
at the finish line.
Or the execution, which the people love
even more than the races,
but this one
is so cool and brutal that half
of the firing squad
turn their eyes away. . . .
Or a picnic in the grass,
where eros kills your appetite.
Or the bullfight where, contrary

to your expectations, the thrill
will be in seeing the matador die,

and lie there, suspended in space,
transported from the ring
into eternity, seized
in the instant the energy goes out of him.
You will not see the man being gored.
You will not even see the bull.

Flowers in a crystal vase.
Pinks, impatiens, clematis,
they'll take you away from sorrow.

A man, a woman, and at the end
of the path, a bench
in the garden with no one
sitting on it and not waiting
anymore for the man
who painted it, a bench freed
finally from human suffering—
allowed to be a bench!
Indifferent to the cares
of anyone who will sit there
hereafter, its real life
transplanted onto the canvas
framed and hung,
like the dead toreador,
like death, who makes
his presence known only
by his absence and by
the absence of his signs,
blood, shadows, darkness,
or the train you will never see again
pulling into the station,
disappearing. . . .

This brutality of what is missing:
this is the key!
The end of the street opens up
into the street you cannot see,

the fabric of the hidden light
flows, folds, unravels,
as the street wakes.

How naked flesh repels the touch
and Berthe Morisot, in repose,
floating on the brown velvet sofa's
lush surface, austere, sensual,
covered from head to toe
but for her hands (and the fan
loosely held in her right hand)
draws you in.

And from this woman there is no escape.

You will die for her.
And never know the bitterness of regret.
You will die for her. Out of desire.
The bars in the Gare St. Lazare
are put there for your protection.
And if you have to fall,
fall toward, not away,
from what you want.
Don't let her slip through
the trellised arbor
or go beyond the grove
that remains inside the frame.
Don't let her go.

1

It's a little later. And very dark and quiet now.
A few scattered lights penetrate the empty distance.

City emptiness terrifies—even without the stars.
I mean—the blankness—and silence—have force: gravity.

"Cold conditions," a fire in the abandoned warehouse.
Abandoned quarries: cold smoke flows out of chiselled rocks like
    fog.

Wind from the east and from the west. Shuddering.
The crowd shuddering to think. And underneath, the earth
    heaving.

And driven: pounding my head through the wall.
Blood throb. And to end again in unknowing.

2

It is this craving, no that isn't it,
this *this*, and only, nothing more or less.

The one who says I will, the one who says I won't.
In what way are they different?

A movement of the mind is a live garden.
Put off by a thousand unwelcome thoughts.

Early morning. The air still dark. Neighborhood hookers,
clipping coupons in the street, enter the supermarket.

An inhabited, haunted mind.
Careworn, cablegrammed, jammed—

At the intersection—

I wander miles. Lose my way.
Coming home after dark every street is a garden.

3

Once the time goes, it's gone.
And no wisdom can retrieve it.

Grave thoughts bear the mind down.
The body has no choice but to follow.

It comes down to yes or no, with pain in back of
every choice that turns to act.

What I find in the night, other than darkness.
In the darkness, other than light.

Solace. What a lovely word.
Solstice. What a lovely word.

4

Cement doesn't count. It doesn't even
remember. It can't even tie its shoe.

Mannequin in gray-blue light. No illusion.
No mere overcoat tossed on a hatrack.

That we cannot see but hear the hammering below.
These are priorities.

Shouts out of nowhere surrounded by elemental
harmonies. Carburetors and exhausts.

Yesterday was centuries ago. Today is all
I know will never go away.

Today when the light slides,
divides and reunites.

5

If we proceed by contraries we keep pace with the waves,
breaking on the way in, whispering on the way out.

Nothing without something to spring unpredictably—
whitecaps, heat lightning, flint-fire, avalanches. . . .

Some semblance of hell is needed to remind us of what is:
sounds of lost souls risen from rubber bodies.

Up all night at the Blackjack table in Las Vegas.
Or was it Reno? I only remember—I stopped in time.

No rest. Only the thought of rest. A thought—grasped,
taking flight from an orange crate with the Hudson's tide. . . .

And so no matter how bad, *is* is better than not.
And long for summer having nothing else to long for.

I think I remember Chicago through the open doors
of boxcars in the railroad yard just below
my bedroom window,

the light, flowing through, drawing me out,
the cold and shadows warning me away,
the times I noticed

one car had been exchanged for another,
or that the same car had inched
forward or backward

along the track: these small changes
were more mysterious than the departure
of the loaded cars

filled with live cattle or dead beef. . . .
And I was tuned into this strangeness
because I was a stranger,

an exile, schooled in reversals: I would run
out of the apartment at night and hide
in the barracks

and beg the MP on duty not to tell
my stepfather I was there, if he came, as he would,
to drag me home.

And because I was a stranger I trusted strangers.
November nights: the wind, howling in the windows,
dragged leaves noisily,

(as if a microphone had been attached to them)
along the pavement after ripping them off the branches,
dragged me out of doors,

toward the lights and wires that made the moon pale.
It must have been November because I wore a leather jacket
lined with flannel

and blue jeans rolled up over motorcycle boots,
and it was not too cold for these escapes to lead
to frostbite and gangrene.

I was ready to risk death, but not another beating
on the dark streets where no one walked, as if prairie stretched
between the rows of charred high rises.

Prairie and rubble lots filled with weeds and stones.
I wondered where the people were in this city of millions.
Inside.

ANY ONE BONE YOU WANT

It's too late to reconsider origins
at this hour or even to
scramble up the hill
toward cemetery shade;
already seeds have taken hold
of the air, the wind
bodies them forth
in imitation of being if
being is to drift
and stay on course; if,
in the release offered
by the proposition, I were to
fly I would die
by heat of summer's hand;

somewhere I read the dead never ache
and that all our curiosity
had to do with ourselves;
suspicions confirmed;
and I believed her when
marching up Broadway, after
a fit of pique, she announced,
"somewhere I read of a bone store
in the neighborhood
where you can get whole skeletons too";
come morning, waking in the heat,
the you I see walking by me
in slow dissolve
moves out of the frame,
and something else takes your place
and wavers in that vacancy:
Any one bone you want.

PERSPECTIVE

They talk about lying to tell the truth.
Whoever "they" are.
To tell the truth—is painful—
in the face of clocktowers—
invisible—in the black rain—
and my Kodak black and whites
do not replicate those sinuous
mountains that look like mountains,
far off, and the hills dotted with hills,
bent, like haybales—
not to dissolve the question
in the matter of "perspective"
or diminish the fertile beauty
of all that flickering in the vineyards
and olive groves,
slow, heavy,
oozing, pouring,
like honey from a jar:
nothing more useless than impatience here;
or the plotting of charts and courses
beyond the present—
splitting the atom with the instant's scimitar,
harmlessly, arm in arm,
drinking from fountains,
dunking, bathing in fountains,
and still to tell the truth was—
is—all that mattered.
Lying played no part in it.

BEFORE GOING TO SEE DA VINCI'S DRAWINGS I SEE A POSTCARD OF HIS THE INFANT IN THE WOMB

It makes you wonder, in the beginning
or the end (of the beginning),
if the skeletal design,

if globe and cosmos do not come down
to *this*:

And if structural density—
the carnivorous exactitude of jaw
genitalia, mouth, sphincter, and nerves
twitching up the spine—
were not destiny and
what we see:
bare trees, the grid
of streets.

Looking at Leonardo's drawing made it hurt
to look at other people, even
a lovely woman moving through the next room.

The skeleton beneath the skin
is nothing compared
to the fine wiring around it.

To be alive, then, to see
what your eyes are seeing with
must by nature be
to feel more pain
than pleasure.

THE RUIN REVIVED

1/ First Glances

It's close to midnight and we've walked
as many miles as the day has hours,
past the tomb of Augustus rising at dusk,
its cypresses and shadows and crouching cats,
at this late hour
the city more awake than ever:

and we are getting used to getting lost
as a way of being—as long as we have
squid with lemon and olive oil to revive us—
and the moon, the full moon,
pocked and radiant over
the still furious and surging Tiber,

and hidden in the river weeds
a man fishing from its banks. . . .
You say a man? You see a figure
crouched with a long pole extending;
a bundle of rags; no face, no hands.

Consolation. . . : the straight, yet dignified
statues of poets like Belli, and the moon
in Trastevere where there's more gaiety
than here, near Santa Maria del Popolo
where Nero's tomb keeps watch

as a ragamuffin puts his fingers
through the sockets of the marble skeleton
set in the wall and leers,
and my unseen neighbor down the hall calls out:
"It's alright with just my shutter locked, right?"

only to keep us awake all night
with an operatic orgasm
that echoes in the courtyard—
whose acoustics rise to the occasion
to rival the Baths of Caracalla—

to where a dozen pairs
of closed white shutters stare. . . .

2/ *The Baths of Caracalla*

This is the exact spot where Shelley wrote *Prometheus Unbound*.
He, like ourselves, arrived too late to get into the Protestant
Cemetery one morning. Could he have forseen he would stay
forever there? Here, in the Baths of Caracalla, I think of whitened
creek-beds—though a hefty crew of laborers is hammering bleachers
for the night's opera when the ruin revives. I didn't have to ask the
two English women why they were at the gate of the Protestant
Cemetery an hour after the unannounced closing time. All is chaos
and delight. I never sit still long enough to write. The *where* never
mattered less. One direction, a step at a time, is two directions,
because it contains the one left behind.

3/ *Rome*

What you must understand
is that it is not Caravaggio's
St. Peter or the Vatican,
nor is it the courtyard in the parking lot
where we eat pollo diavolo and fresh calamari
under the sign of the pitchfork
under the sign "Ostaria La Capannina"
looking at the two-in-the-afternoon
rolled down shutters on the Piazza della Coppella,
where a gray haired man with a grizzled beard
in a tee shirt and army fatigues clutches a can
of "Fanta," and the local cats come over
in homage to possibility, and we are grateful
for the coolness of the shadows on the paving stones
a mere block from where the crowd plunges,
on armored feet! It is not basilicas,
crowds, the whirling of starlings,
not the marble galleries or the clay floors of the catacombs
where the Christians used to hide from the Romans,
not the variety of Christs—
the classic emaciate to the bloodless ones,

not Caravaggio's young St. Peter
who mocks your gaze by looking through your eyes,
not masterpieces or competent pictures,
the gracious or the cranky, ease or exhaustion,
not, not denial, nothing, then, other than what is.

4/ Recovering from Michelangelo

For who can decipher the woman
in Adam's bent knee with neck craned upward and strain-
ing. For who can penetrate
the meticulous design, or all the seeming,
as Jonah, emerging from the whale's vaginal mouth,
explodes into relief, and the snake
holding Eve against the tree is
the tree. Light is revelation. For all
aspires to rise, as the saved haul
themselves out of hell. The fall is time.
Which is why Charon waits with such confidence.
Light is what I want to escape from now—
at two in the afternoon.

So many cameras aimed at the separation
of the finger of God and the finger of Adam!
And yet it is equally fine—and this is the key—
to walk the city in the later
afternoons and evenings as it is to squint
at a thousand pictures. The world-stage surfaces.
You consult the map to get us to the Via Paradiso
through the Via Doloroso.
And where there are no bridges reflections
bear us across. Without you
I would be doubly lost.

5/ Lines Written on the Via Veneto

Wandering through the ruins of this ruined city,
sacked so many times it can hardly stand,
looking through the eyeholes of monuments
leading to worn stone and sky,
I thought I was another,

I thought I must be someone else or elsewhere.
And mourning doves nestled in the eaves
of the arches over the Borghese garden,
and children cantered past on ponies,
the same children I would have seen
if I had been here before
but those children are now the ones
walking the ponies, holding the reins,
not riding them.
Only the warped and pitted statues
have grown older, the sky and the clouds.
Ten years ago I didn't believe all things
changed this way—by degrees—
and if someone had told me
I would have argued myself hoarse
and toppled home, spent,
into an empty bed.

6/ Verticals

A girl sitting in front of me at Il Palio, on the Campo in Siena, overlooking the Palazzo. She has her back to me but I can see her breast through her sleeveless dress. I am placed here, it is placed there, small, round, and full. She writes with her left hand. She is talking to another girl at the same table, her friend. She draws a tower in the air over the Torre del Manga. She does not pause at the gargoyles poised to leap or the martins perching, disappearing into square holes, who launch themselves from the fearful faces of the stone she-wolves. Her hair is short and sun-bleached. And her breast hangs like forbidden fruit, pendulous, untouchable. She is only a girl. And I am only still a boy in my mother's eyes. The need to touch. The desire to touch. More erotic than sexual. Everywhere in Italy, this summer and on the walls of old basilicas, the laying on of hands. Mary holds Christ. And Christ, in Duccio's painting, washes the feet of his disciples—not at all austerely. Summer and the body. Hers, mine. This is all I see in a thousand towns and countries. This is the sweetest hour of the day or night.

7/ *In Siena*

The Just have a slender chance.
Only twittering survives.
Witness these martins over Palazzo Publico
disappearing into square holes,
launching themselves
from the gargoyles whose unfaded expressions
find relief only in stone
as the shadows dwindle to darkness
on the Campo as the day slows
to a miraculous halt.

In the blighted frescoes
where Lorenzetti's devils
order the torn-out
faces of the innocent
to perform unendurable acts,
the best parts of the story
have been destroyed:
whether by negligence,
weather, or will,
this witness cannot tell.

8/ *Milan*

Watching an old beggar in a Navy blue greatcoat. 85 degrees and
sultry. He has been standing there for as long as I've been sitting
here, milling about as if waiting for a bus, but one bus, and another
bus comes and he's still there, pacing the sign. Twenty minutes
have passed, and a hundred couples have walked by where he's
standing, turning and turning, slowly and absolutely, like a bear in
a shooting gallery. He hasn't shaved for days. He has no hair to
comb, except around the temples. He might have been given the
Medal of Honor for bravery in World War II and look at him now.
The world owes him nothing. His coat is buttoned to the top. It's
all he has on. My father used to say that drinking hot tea in the
heat was the best way to keep cool. The more you sweated the
cooler you would be. His greatcoat could be the only air-cooled
outfit in Milan, where a G string and a halter sell for 400,000 lire

in a store where a naked mannequin sits with her feet up and legs crossed on the soft tan leather sofa in the window.

9/ *Foreshortening*

Mantegna's Christ
looks more like a man
than one of the sons
of God: The toes
of the right foot
are clenched, the feet hang
over the bed.

No levity, no gravity, no attitude
can cover for the body,
prone to fatigue,
at last released, a final
heaviness crawling the limbs
to be watered there,
at last, by tears.

A sheet, a chest cavity.
That a man should lie there,
uncomfortable and dead,
and let women cry over him.

10/ *Last Morning*

Streets of Milan, the ultimate hustle bustle, the final mercantile. Not a leaf in sight—as far as Castello Sforzecsa. This street rings with the turbulence of traffic, the angst of impending departure. The banks take away . . . and add to the noise and knottedness of the crowd. Leonardo, Stendahl: both came to live here of their own free will. But that was before the invention of the Exhaust Fume. A restless black cat skirmishes back and forth under the chairs. There is no haven for him in Milan, on this island between Via San Prospero and Via Dante. Would he rest content on the Corriere Della Sera if I wedged my copy under a leg of this chair once I am gone? Is this a just end for Michel Foucault's obituary? Is it true that we cannot gauge the degree of another's sexual pleasure? Foucault was obsessed by the repercussions of this. I read *Madness and Civilization* in the days when I still underlined, darkening most of its pages. . . . Now the birds, crowded out of the sky by high fashion, disappear, this Monday morning, just before noon and, as if the city were a prison yard, two teenage boys rev up a motor scooter attempting to break out. The absence of the sun is a hunger of mind pure as the cat's restlessness. Whatever rumbles under the grating will some day be delivered.

11/ In Ravenna

The light comes out of tombs:
Dante, Theodoric, Galla Placida,

and the blue of mosaics
mocks heaven,

that stern, final judge.
The Romans, Byzantium,

all have gone the way
of history, as birds sing

outside the vaults,
and the archangels,

unmoving, call
witnesses to the altar:

strangers, those
of foreign tongues,

and in the end,
children.

12/ Venice: The Monks

Solemnly they flee, beyond sense and care
and the reward after, toward shadows, escaping
the heat of the afternoon, toward what lies
on the other side of the trees, vanishing

as fear shatters the order of events and I
walk the sun-hardened Venetian stones,
hoping for a clearing breeze on the canal
to lift the heat and sultriness.

THE WHY LIGHT

What remains after the smoke.
What is a city for other than to be sacked.
What remains after the light
on the ruins and the outcrop stone.
What remains of the light after the light.

What remains of the body on the stairs.
Why must the light retain
its clarity over so much desolation.
Why does the light shine equally on the lie
and on the other lie, the truth.

I cannot conceive
of the loneliness of the grass
in this windswept place without us.
The messenger bears the dead boy's body
in the fullness of the light.

Smoke through broken fences.
Around Andromache, a ring of women.
She cries out for everyone to hear,
sorrow no one's possession.

You cry out where no one can hear you.

Last night, rocking the baby to sleep,
    I thought of Italy and of you there.
He grows wide-eyed toward midnight.
    All I could think about was the light
as if the bad weather had roosted and calcified
    under my eyelids. Now the sky is as blue
as a blue wall, peeling, with layers
    of posters underneath, as blue
as the Virgin's robe in Giotto's frescoes.
    And, leaning against the wall,
an old man talks of cicadas and crickets
    and a young man talks of history. . . .
The sweetness of the light this morning
    parallels that of towns whose names
ending in "o"—Urbino, Arezzo, Orvieto—
    and railway platforms I memorized from train windows.
And the transcontinental language of the cradle. . . .

Impossible for a man to escape
    over these furrowed fields,
like the rabbits in Uccello's *Battle of San Romano*. . . .
    What is not always being reenacted?
Spring now in Rome: The ancient world
    throws off its wrappings and teaches voyagers
from the New World how to idle or die,
    how to wait without fuming, teaches without
instruction. Commerce never hedges. Tiber and Seine
    flow through their cities.
Moving on a parallel line the Hudson can remain unseen.
    Many who come here never see it.
And never see the Japanese plum mount its guard.
    Winter we have endured, and the waiting.
Now a child. Exhaustion, relief. Waiting is worse
    than the effort, the upheavel of being born.
Now we awaken to his cries and cat nap between them.

THE MYSTERY IN THE GARDEN

(After a visit to Marion Lerner Levine's
studio at Yaddo and her painting in
progress, *The Mystery in the Greenhouse*)

The letter pinned to the wall,
unfolding, telling
of forgotten disasters,
sunken ships, desperate messages.
The drawers, yanked out of the chest:
a fragile tilt, an incline,
and everything is askew—
upturned in rows like gravestones.
The bold handwriting,
"I did not expect
this tragedy to occur
while I was here. . . ."
The story hidden inside
the arbitrary forms and shapes
and colors of the past.
The quiet and longing
for a time in the garden:
three women in the garden,
as battleships gather
in the harbor just before
the first World War.
The terrible stillness
that precedes mystery.

It looked so peaceful in the garden
if there had been a door
I would have walked in, a gate
and I would have opened it.

She is standing in a red dress
at the entrance to the Botanical Gardens
in early spring.
Smell of magnolias in blossom,
sticky, hot, white.
Gestures, the sound

of another's voice
in a time when sound mattered.

Railroads, semaphores
in the smoky night,
clang of the garden gate,
and the torn letter, unforgotten.

Arrivals, departures.
Gardens and mazes.

I enter without fear of getting lost,
keen on finding a way.

A way . . .

It is not a place
from where I would need
to be released to live!
Further and father!

Enter here under the garden's gaze.
Amazed, enter the maze.

To be, finally,
where you have always been.
Enter with delight.

The real past, waiting, this cold spring,
for irises and violets and magnolias.
The mystery unfolding
in the longing of J for J,
anxiety, ancient suspicions:

"Don't let him do to you
what he did to me,"
were her words in September, 1934 . . .

Indecipherable signatures.
Cryptic, meticulous vision.

To preserve the actual,
but first to enter
the garden, abandoned,
abandoning all habits
and the sundered doubles
of other habits,
gnawing under the skin
like marbleized light—
to enter, then, without fear
of where you will end.

The real, the actual,
flickering, pulsing,
oblivious to the dampness,
raw and awful,
like the skeleton inside the flesh
wearing away desire,
whirling turmoil out of nothing
and no-things,
not what the eye gathers without the ear,
seared, scarred like the fields,
scored like the sky by fire.

The garden, the rows
of gravestones under the arch
where the ducks hide,
lace, latticework,
flowing
like the spirit reclaimed.

I want the murmuring I hear to become flesh,
to lacerate the air.
Sometimes I imagine the earth is still.
And it takes a cracked cup
with a landscape like this one
running through it
to help the light settle down
where it can see,
through these still lives,
eternity,

glimpsed like lightning
disappearing
over the next mountain,

to wander the forbidden ground.

Sound of all that falling.
Father gone, home alone, flees to the sun.
So long since I have seen the sun.
can I vouch for what it was?
Would my testimony hold?
Would anyone listen, much less believe?
The sun I love, warming my heart,
warming my hands.
Can't hoard the fire.

Father gone, nobody home,
everything far away
and terrifying, like forked light,
far away, scorching
the rooftiles of the chosen,
and the amber turquoise
stained glass windows
of St. Clement's Church
where I wandered
in a haze of transcendence
that Easter Sunday,
and the women were murmuring,
bright eyes flashing,
laughter flowing,
entering a garden's maze,
aroused, and beckoning:
enter here under the garden's gaze.

SOLSTICE

Beginning in mourning. And not because,
as Breughel says, the world is unfaithful.
Beginning in grief. And not because
the sea recedes for miles
at low tide and the muck rises and hisses
and you walk not too carefully out and out
as though the water were meant never to return,
as though you would not drown if it did return,
as though anyone could escape double solitude,
being alone together and the edge
that is the opposite of death
and yet inspires the longing
for numbness, indifference, stone.

It begins on a day without rain after weeks of rain.
Someone is waking. Eyes scan the darkened room.
It is morning and it cannot be morning.
Palm rubs warmth into palm.
It is a subway stalled on the edge of a gorge
where the rain has washed away the tracks.
Someone awakes in a sleeping car
after a long night without sleep
wondering, where am I?
No newspapers, no telephones.
Slowly light filters down the hillside,
cascading over rocks, thistles, weeds. . . .

Mist binds the shaggy branches of the fir trees.
No paths anywhere, and when you look down
it is too steep to breathe and thunder
is already rough and tumble in the clouds,
as though there were no escape, as though
you did not know there is no *as though*,
as though the chill you felt itself did not tremble
and you did not shudder inwardly
to see the fire haunted trees and know lightning
had been there before.

There is nothing left:
no hole into the other world,
no undeniable spark,
no atom tossed up by the breakers
left to smolder in the driftwood: nothing.
Not even the smoke from last night's fires,
not even the memory of this summer
that is still passing, not done.
Not Vega, though it ripples
with possibilities, or the full moon
searching the branches for traces and signs:
we know what was.
We have to deal with what is.
Or be left, as it were, in the flood
of intergalactic activity
bordering on a trace of life,
out to dry,
like the eagle's feather I.found
in the dust of the roadside,
a potential quill, an arrow:
there is no time.
And that's the least of it.
The beach, littered with shells,
cracked, every one of them,
does not, cannot, console,
anymore than the night sky,
bursting with light, blinding us,
has the wit to see what it
mindlessly reveals,
though I would hazard that the owls,
yes, in particular the owls,
take what the light is saying for
what it's worth, without hesitating,
when it feels right, to blink.
But to have known what to ask—
that surpasses wisdom.
Not to mistake the burning

in the early morning and evening,
dispatching first darkness
then shadows, for fire.

AUGUST IS NOT A MONTH

1

The season, to speak in the language of seasons,
is ending, and sweetly—with breezes.

The summer, which season it was, is ending
more sadly than any season will ever end.

Pity—is a human mechanism.
And the body has its own time.

And the black bear falling
out of the pine tree

falls endlessly, prisoner of air—
of bars that stretch beyond the range of cells.

2

What hollow is not a grave?
What empty space? The earth

a hole, a passageway, with orbit
as a kind of falling off, falling away,

which the day, with its shadows, imitates,
and we, tied to distances, mimic.

September's crystal skies, bleak
ecstasy in the heights over rusty fields. . . .

No, I haven't lowered my expectations:
I've learned what not to expect.

3

And the freshness in the air
this morning after rain, the way

everything glistens, as though everything
were forgotten, even if it is,

the cruelty or disinterest of water,
reducing all news, all information,

to a mood, the baby knocking her head
against the stairs, crying, her mother

rising, the stanzas in Blok's Ravenna
going on about the sea erasing

all signs of life from mossy sepulchres, the sea—
eating away eternity.

4

Dread at the edge of vision,
no longer mired in the strategems

of the self, or its weather, *the* weather.
And a hawk on a branch can prey.

Waiting is action. *Medaglia d'Oro* on
the stove quickens the listless afternoon.

Lying back in bed afterwards she says, "It's either
rain or pine needles falling on the roof."

The dark coming earlier by the day,
to say nothing of the hour, to say.

A kind of dread. The mere end of summer . . .
happens every year, wherever you are, and yet. . . .

The one thing these New England
villages lack is a square.

And yet—if I had some money
I'd stay the whole year.

5

There's always the chance there might be time
to begin, "Loin des oiseaux, des troupeaux,"

when the village girls disappear into the heather . . .
Another answer might slip unnoticed through the sluices.

Ladislas might be granted a passport.
Lulu, who hasn't had a drink in ten years

(though, in her own words, "still an alcoholic"),
could begin to conceive of life as a

"gift" rather than a "job."
There's always the chance, once the locks

have been changed after the potlatch
(which cured our homesick possessions),

after the glasses have been converted to sand,
the wallpaper into birches, sound into cellos

and Madonnas into goldfinches, that someone
might hear, among the lightning fireflies,

among the harebells, in the same season
as this one, under Sirius, beckoning

wind in the stillness, wondering
what animal left these tracks. . . .

RUNNING OUT

Not much time left   here   in the other Brooklin
    overlooking   Herrick Bay
driven like an anchor into the town's center

it is as though all of the animals had come out of the woods
    to speak   now   in that instant   when the season   flees
and leaves its shards in the middens

the black bear, the gray coyote, the broad-tailed hawk
who all summer have been so
    assiduously hiding   appear

my neighbor   won't go out of her house alone
and when the full moon hangs low in the branches
    and doesn't   annihilate the stars

there's nowhere to hide   from its cold pallor
all stands exposed   osmotic hunks   creatures who breathe
    so when a man staggers red-faced and drunk up Naskeag Road

in the direction of town and blunders into a woman's house
through   an unlocked door   looking for help
    late one Sunday afternoon   he's done for

and the signs of damage are the skidmarks and the gold
    Volkswagon beetle   a once souped-up job
fuming in the roadside bushes   and going farther

and farther into the woods every time the story is told . . .

and yesterday, at dusk, while the last shadows
    were holding their ground against the spreading redness
I paused by Arthur Smith's, whose house stands

on the level after the steepest hill
    in the world. And I said, "Hi Arthur,
how're ya doin'?" "Better today.

Gettin' better every day. By the time I reach a-hundred
      I ought to be a man." And poked his fork
into some meat on the grill, shook his head and said:

"Not quite done yet . . ." Just beyond, the harbor
      was packed with boats and cars lined up on the side
of the road. It could have been Singapore.

CIPHER

Some gnostic text asks
what can we, man, hope for
in our fallen condition,
and though I don't subscribe
to any shibboleths or hold
to any superstition, I wonder.
The sages in the trees
whisper by the breezes
and swear, what you once
called August is autumn.
Feel the bite in the air,
the chill in the canals
and estuaries,
fleeing, don't ask what:
this light lasts an instant
like your life,
and you, turning the pages
of your newspaper
never see how tenaciously
the shadows stay
before they are erased
by the dark;
the broad-tailed hawk tests
that branch like an acrobat
and free-falls over the sedge
before swiftly ascending the spruces;
the black bear
wads up the hedgehog's fur
and leaves it tangled in the kelp
and driftwood on the beach
without a track;
what riotous
unrequited creatures
go into the vegetable rows,
searching for corn
when storms are predicted.

TERRESTRIAL MARKS

> This emptiness of sky and water
> and these very faint terrestrial
> marks (a boat, a promontory)
> which float there . . . the blue of
> the sky, the gray of the sea, the
> pink of the dawn.
>
> *ROLAND BARTHES*

1

Arrival, at last,
the road unrolled,
the silence listing,
the cold and fog welcome. . . .

Arrival, moon in pines,
illuminated gravel.
Absence of jackhammers
the final shock.

This part of the story
is always the same:
Begin by getting
the place in order.

Get from here to there
by ladder only.
Arrival
no final

redemption,
any more than
gull cry
signifies love.

2

Two boats are overturned, and a ripple
beyond the farthest boat and not yet
in the sight of the houses lined up

on the beach suggests that someone
is drowning. . . . The sun is high—
over the houses, the treetops, gone.
The trees blaze red orange red.
The boats wash up along the beach
and face the houses on the other shore.
The only people on this canvas
are either disembodied, severed, or drowning:
there only through absence.
As you are here.

3

Huddled on the rocks in Maine, reading *The Trojan Women* in
the dawn, low tide, thrum of lobster boats, small islands in fog,
shells and kelp strewn at my feet, and the cut in these rocks
images a medieval fortress: mussel shells cupped like sentinels or
gargoyles on the battlements, turbaned snails propped like skulls
along the edges, tide pools make small moats. Rocks like turtles'
backs. Distant cry of gulls. Beyond what islands I cannot see. . . .
A cormorant skims the water and cuts across the coastline in swift,
crisp diagonals. The sound of motors comes near, the islands
appear. A lobster boat darts sideways, up and down in the cove,
like a spider building its web. Now everything I have seen or
invented this morning: the shells, cormorants, even the fortress,
is gone. The edge of the visible, gone too, as the horizon flattens
out, annihilated by light. And the sound of an engine is drawn
across my line of vision by a small white boat, and the shadow of
wings that cross as they cut across my shadow: the only thing
that stays.

Words have never been adequate.
They are all we have ever had.
But we know what Euripides meant when he said
count no man happy until he's dead.

4

It is morning, in the veins and in the blood,
hunkered in some rocks,
fog already lifted, most audible sound

a voice like Tokyo Rose on a ship's radio
bouncing off the water from miles offshore.
The morning after,—and I missed
the Independence Day Parade. . . .
Soon to be the day after and there's so little time.
It is good not to hear about the executions of
"rebel parties" and "terrorist activities". . . .
For a few days, that is.
And good, for a short time, to conjure an image
not of this time but of this place,
as when, one morning last January,
we followed Caravaggio's woods
into the deep space inside the canvas,
(past the pond where someone's reflection
had already plunged), hidden,
like infinity, by too much artificial light.
Too much light. . . . It is light that makes
some sheep asleep in these crevices blend
with the rocks' black, white, and coral veins.
And stay out of sight.

5 / *Enter Gulliver*

This morning the sea's quiet as a lake.
Ants set siege to the citadel at my feet:
They scale the walls, prowl the turrets,
overrun the keep, and drag off no plunder.
Tide's going out. There's still plenty of water
in the small moats at the base of this
granite bouldered fortress. Kelp clings
like ivy to its walls, rope down which lovers
can escape to a rendevous in the forest and,
climbing up, invaders can invade. The water's quiet,
but some cackling laughter from a sailboat
carries island to island.
What could be so funny at this hour of the morning?
Up for two hours, I'm not yet awake.
The sun is warm, not hot, on my forehead.
The day is not yet lost! The rusty lichens sprawl
like an aerial view of terra cotta roofs
on a hilltop town in Italy

Should I appeal to all of the absent gods,
spare us, spare us, let us be delivered,
or should I take the repetition of the cicadas' shrill note
or the thrushes' song as a response?
Do birds still carry messages from the gods?
Not, I imagine, if invoked with a small *g*.
Plash of oars, flash of aluminum on the blade . . .
out of water it glares and blinds. . . .
A woman, on the rock adjacent to this one,
across a dip in the terrain of marshy grass
and jagged rock too difficult to cross in a straight
line, rises, a baby in her arms who lets out a sound
that is either a desperate cry or hoot of delight.
And it is my turn to take him.

6

As the visible recedes, something else takes over:
Beating a retreat toward the horizon line and
vanishing point the fog uncovers a new new world,
though there is no boat or man poling a barge
through a rock cavern to affirm the human on this shore.
The snails are snails, the pebbles pebbles, the kelp—
good to put over mussels to keep them fresh and cool
in the bucket. . . . But, to keep the log accurate,
a man sitting on a rock, his hand moving from left to right
looks and listens so intently you'd think
he was part of the landscape and more
an image of the human than a boat on the point,
its masts down and wound in burlap like scrolls.

7 / *The Crossing*

Midsummer dusk in Ellsworth. Two boys duck under the bridge of
the Union River across from the Union Trust Savings Bank. They
prowl the shallows, fishing with their hands. Waiting for my wife
and three month old son to emerge from John Edwards' Natural
Food store with Danish coffee and Canadian Sourdough, I am
standing under the awning of the Hancock County Auditorium on
Main Street in the old part of town. Here, there's still more clap-
board and brick than sheet rock and cinder block, next to The

Mex where a man-sized plastic bullfrog slops a yellow tongue across his chops in a gravel garden. The two boys move in a cautious circle as if each held the end of a net which, merely by lifting it, they would pull out a hundred trout and bass. I've never seen anyone fish that river before. Maybe it's the season or the hour. The two boys stalk the shallows, with delicate pauses, alert to the drama that precedes the kill. The one facing me dives and comes up shrieking as the brown trout, speckled in the sun's last rays, spurts out of his clasped hands, returning, with a quiet splash, to water. The white spire of the Congregational Church climbs above the other signs as the sky darkens. The boys narrow their circle, eager to begin again.

8 / *The Lighthouse*

Where are you now, arriving or leaving?
The morning tokens other surprises:
light glittering on the lighthouse as if
wind had sanded down its walls for years.
I want to say—"this landscape"—
but it is not a landscape; it is the sea;
a flat hourglass set to rescue the abandoned
lighthouse that has lost its hold on the soil,
its balance, since we were here;
and now, in the noon sun,
the lighthouse flashes and flares
sending what messages where
no eye can make it out in the dazzle:
only the light, the glare;
and the dry, spindly trees
below would flee the fire;
and heat sprawls over the high weeds
in the meadow where bees drowse
in the wild roses and the raspberries,
and the children play chase-the-goat on the paths. . . .
Better not to say; better to beam in on
colors the baby can see; reds and yellows;
beam in on—then rest content: Better than
to be content only when rest-
less; arriving; or leaving.

9 / *A Sequel*

A sequel: no cargo, no absolutes,
no travel or distances.
Here's an island without a lighthouse.
Abandon appearances.

Where can desire
spend itself without a cliff,
windly bluff, and a sun-
stricken lighthouse. . . ?

The sky gathers in the window
and far out at sea—
a black shred
that wants to swallow me.

In the sequel there are no people:
the seascape, raucous squawks,
the caretaker's tarpaper shack
roof caved in dead center

on both sides of the stovepipe;
garden of overgrown goldenrod,
with a panda doll propped
against inner tubes;

and, in strict formation on Hog Island,
battalions of pine spears . . .
so that what happens in the sequel
happens offstage,

in a room only a few feet
from the street and noise
of the city; a room
(and is there ever a reason

to leave?) where the story
stranded its characters,
known to us by the pink granite
paperweight on their desk,

cigar boxes filled
with curious shells, remnants,
and by their far away looks—
no windows.

Mark Rudman was born in New York City and spent his boyhood and youth in the Midwest and West. He graduated from the New School for Social Research in 1971 and received an M.F.A. from the School of the Arts at Columbia University in 1974. His poetry has been widely published in such journals as *The Atlantic Monthly, Harper's, Ironwood,* and *The Paris Review*, and such anthologies as *Intro, The Random Review*, and the *New Directions Annual*. He has received an Ingram Merrill Fellowship for the long poem *By Contraries*, a P.E.N./Columbia Translation Center Fellowship, and a CCLM Editor's Award. He is the author of *In the Neighboring Cell* and two chapbooks, *The Ruin Revived* and *The Mystery in the Garden*. He is also the author of *Robert Lowell: An Introduction to the Poetry* and the translator of Pasternak's *My Sister— Life* and *The Sublime Malady* for which he received the Max Hayward Award. He now lives with his wife and son in New York City where he teaches in the Writing Program at New York University and at York College. He is the editor of *Pequod*.

ABX5277   4/3/89